DIARY PRACTICING VIPASSANA & THE FOUR FOUNDATIONS "OF MINDFULNESS SUTTA

Ven. Dr. Bhikṣuṇī TN Gioi Huong

Diary
PRACTICING VIPASSANA
&
THE FOUR FOUNDATIONS OF MINDFULNESS SUTTA

Ven. Dr. Bhikṣuṇī TN Gioi Huong

TON GIAO PUBLISHING

Huong Sen Buddhist Temple
19865 Seaton Avenue

Perris, CA 92570, USA
Tel: 951-657-7272, Cell: 951-616-8620

Email: huongsentemple@gmail.com

thichnugioihuong@yahoo.com

https://www.facebook.com/Huong.Sen.Riverside

Web: www.huongsentemple.com

CONTENTS

PREFACE

On the Majjhima Nikaya (No. 10) and the Digha Nikaya (No. 22), the Buddha taught the Four Foundations of Mindfulness Sutta (Satipaṭṭhāna Sutta). It is a basic, core sutta that helps to transform negative minds into pure ones in a highly effective and quick way.

The Four Foundations of Mindfulness are mindfulness of body, feelings, mind, and Dhamma. These four places comprise the entire field of human experience and are places where practitioners constantly remember and observe.

Vipassana is the insight wisdom to observe the objects of the four categories (body, feelings, mind, Dhamma) as they are. The practitioner will scan that all phenomena, oneself, others, and the whole world are always arising and passing away, and will realize that this reflects impermanence, suffering, and non-self characteristics.

Reflecting on the body as impure.

Reflecting on feelings as suffering.

Reflecting on the mind as impermanent.

Reflecting on phenomena as selfless.

These four contemplations are a guide to bring peace and purity to everyone in the world, regardless of skin color or religion, monastic or laypeople. That is the practical and effective message of practicing that the Buddha gave to humanity more than 2,600 years ago. It is still present and practiced all over the world.

There are many Vipassana meditation centers practicing the method of Four Foundations of Mindfulness in India and many countries around the world, among them, the Dhamma Bodhi International Centre. It was founded in 1974[1] by Burmese Meditation Master Satya Narayan Goenka following the tradition of teacher Sayagyi U Ba Khin.

I was fortunate to attend the ten-day course (December 15–26, 2023) at Dhamma Bodhi Meditation School, Bodh Gaya, Bihar State, India. In it, practitioners are instructed to follow the meditation center's rules: keep the five precepts (*avoid killing, stealing, lying, adultery, and drinking alcohol*), and practice the meditation method of observing the breathing in and out right at the nostrils, monitoring emotions, sensations in the body, on feelings... The mind settles and subtly scans to see the movements of the body (the biochemical body)

1. Bodhgaya International Vipassana Meditation Centre, Bodhgaya, Bihar, India, https://bodhi.dhamma.org/

and feelings (the sensations) that are pleasant, difficult, suffering, pain, heat, cold . . . all come and go, back and forth impermanently. The practitioners play the role like a mirror, just observing without any reaction. Gradually, practitioners' minds become calm, peaceful, and deep, without negative anger or hatred; the mind will be purified, clear, and healthy. Slowly and deligently, practitioners progress into the long meditation courses with this higher mind training method, leading to a higher spiritual state. The Buddha concluded in the Four Foundations of Mindfulness Sutta:

Bhikkhus, if anyone should develop these four foundations of mindfulness in such a way for seven years, one of two fruits could be expected of him: either final knowledge here and now, or if there is a trace of clinging left, non-return. . .

Let alone seven years bhikkhus. If anyone should develop these four foundations of mindfulness in such a way for six years... for five years... for one year, one of two fruits could be expected for him: either final knowledge here and now, or if there is a trace of clinging left, non-return...

Let alone one year... let alone half a month... If anyone should develop these four foundations of mindfulness in such a way for seven days, one of two fruits could be expected for him: either final knowledge here and now, or if there is a trace of clinging left, non-return.

This is the direct path for the purification of beings, for the surmounting of sorrow and lamentation, for the disappearance of pain and grief, for the attainment of the true way, for the realization of Nibbana—namely the four foundations of mindfulness.[2]

What this writer saw, heard, learned, understood, practiced, and experienced were written down and compiled into a Vietnamese-English bilingual booklet: **Diary: Practicing Vipassana and the Four Foundations of Mindfulness Sutta.**

We respectfully pay our respects to the Dhamma Bodhi Meditation Center, Bodh Gaya, Bihar, India, for organizing these precious spiritual experience meditation classes for free. We would like to pay our respects to Master Bhikṣuṇī Hai Trieu Am for her appendix of the very thorough and awakened teachings on the Four Foundations of Mindfulness. On this occasion, we also express our sincere thank to Bhante Ratna Buddha, Bhikṣuṇī Viên Nhuận, Bhikṣuṇī Nhuận Tường, Bhikṣuṇī Đức Trí, Bhikṣuṇī Viên Quang, Bhikṣuṇī Tịnh Hỷ, Bhikṣuṇī Pháp Huệ, Ms. Kirby and others who helped to give information, translate, print, proofread, edit and publish the book as well as support for the Vipassana course.

The author enthusiastically shares her experience during the ten days of meditation with readers near and far, and there will certainly be many shortcomings. We respectfully hope that Venerable Monastics and friends will please guide her so that the future editions can be more complete.

The Four Foundations of Mindfulness is the common

---

2. The Middle Length Discourse of the Buddha, translated by Bhikkhu Nanamoli & Bhikkhu Bodhi.

path of all saints and all practitioners.

Diligence, patience, and perseverance are the secrets to success.

May all sentient beings practice Dhamma and Vipassana on body, feelings, mind, and Dhamma until they attain liberation.

Namo Sakyamuni Buddha,

End of year 2023, Bodhgaya, India

Triple Bows,

Ven. Dr. Bhikṣuṇī TN Gioi Huong

Huongsentemple@gmail.com

CHAPTER 1

INTRODUCTION

By the end of 2023, Bodhgaya (India) was bustling with more than 4,000 monastics and lay Buddhists from Southeast Asian countries such as India, Cambodia, Thailand, Sri Lanka, Laos, Vietnam, Indonesia, Bangladesh, Malaysia, and Singapore who had come to attend the Pali Tipitaka Chanting Course under the sacred Bodhi tree on December 2–12, 2023.

After the chanting course, many Vietnamese nuns and Buddhists joined the ten-day meditation course (December 15–26, 2023) at Dhamma Bodhi Meditation Centre organized by the Bodhgaya International Vipassana Meditation Centre, Bodh Gaya, Bihar, India.[3]

3. Bodh Gaya International Vipassana Meditation Centre, Bodhgaya, Bihar, India, https://bodhi.dhamma.org/
(Trung tâm Thiền Tứ Niệm Xứ Quốc tế Bodhgaya, Bồ Đề Đạo Tràng,

I (Bhikṣuṇī TN Gioi Huong), Bhikṣuṇī Tinh Hi, and Bhikṣuṇī Phap Hue also registered to attend this course on the Buddha land after finishing the Pali Chanting Course.

Bhikṣuṇī TN Gioi Huong (standing in center with a scarf and Vietnamese Nuns in front of Dhamma Bodhi Meditation Hall, 2023

bang Bihar, Ấn Độ, https://bodhi.dhamma.org/)

CHAPTER 2

THE EXPERIENCE OF A TEN-DAY VIPASSANA RETREAT

1. BODH GAYA MEDITATION CENTRE

This Vipassana Meditation Centre was founded by the late Myanmar Meditation Master Satya Narayan Goenka, in 1974, following the tradition of the Myanmar teacher, Sayagyi U Ba Khin, based on the Four Foundations of Mindfulness of Shakyamuni Buddha. Currently, there are 150 Vipassana meditation centers of Master Goenka on continents[4] such as Asia (India, Thailand, Ceylon, Burma, Vietnam), America (North America: Canada and the United States, South America: Colombia, Argentina, Brazil), Africa, Europe (United Kingdom, Belgium, Netherlands, Spain) and

4. https://www.dhamma.org/vi/locations/directory#002

Oceania (Australia and New Zealand). This meditation method has immediate and specific benefits for the body and mind. It is valuable in helping all people regardless of religion or skin color, to purify the body and mind, and to reduce stress. Using this ancient technique, the body becomes peaceful, and the mind is calm. It is a key to happiness and the art of living taught by Shakyamuni Buddha in the Four Foundations of Mindfulness Sutta (Satipaṭṭhāna Sutta). Meditation Master U Ba Khin and Master Goenka have succeeded in reviving Buddhist meditation teachings, ensuring their existence and development in the modern twenty-first century.

According to the Vridhamma website,[5] from 1994 onwards, every year 2,500 meditation courses were held at Goenka's meditation centers around the world, and an average of 150,000 meditators (new and old) attended each year under the guidance of 300 meditation masters who were students and assistants of Master Goenka. This number is gradually increasing.

The center organizes many meditation courses for three, eight, ten, twenty, forty-five, and sixty days, depending on the diligent practice process of the meditator and the approval of the guiding meditation teacher.

---

5. https://os.vridhamma.org/Old-Students (phải là thiền sinh cũ, được Ban tổ chức đưa ID và mật mã mới vào được website để lấy thông tin).

2. THE TEN-DAY MEDITATION COURSE

After registering online on the website,[6] the practitioners will receive an email notification of acceptance, and prepare to enter the ten-day meditation retreat. During these ten days, we are required to be absolutely 100 percent silent, completely keeping silence in body, speech, and mind, cutting off all phone or email communication with the outside world. The organizers arrange all for us such as accommodation, meals twice a day, and meditation instruction for ten days completely free of charge. Just register online, and if we meet the eligibility criteria, we will be accepted.

3. TIMETABLE

4:00 a.m.   Morning wake-up bell

4:30 – 6:30 a.m. Meditation in the hall or your room

6:30 – 8:00 a.m. Breakfast break

8:00 – 9:00 a.m. Group meditation in the hall

9:00 –11:00 a.m. Meditation in the hall or your room according to the teacher's instructions

11:00 – 12:00 noon Lunch break

12 noon – 1:00 p.m. Rest and interviews with the teacher

1:00 – 2:30 p.m. Meditate TN in the hall or your room

2:30 – 3:30 p.m. Group meditation in the hall

3:30 – 5:00 p.m. Meditation in the hall or your room

6. https://www.dhamma.org

according to the teacher's instructions

   5:00 – 6:00 p.m. Tea break

   6:00 – 7:00 p.m. Group meditation in the hall

   7:00 – 8:15 p.m. Teacher's discourse in the hall

   8:15 – 9:00 p.m. Group meditation in the hall

   9:00 – 9:30 p.m. Question time in the hall

   9:30 p.m.   Retire to your room – lights out

4. RULES

Practitioners must completely comply with the rules of the meditation center to support concentration. The student's belongings, such as money, documents, cell phones, electronic devices, bells, rosaries, and personal food must be turned over to the organizers before entering the meditation retreat. The organizers have a storage room in which students lock and keep their own keys. Students can only open it after completing the meditation session. We are not allowed to recite Buddha's name, hold a rosary, chant suttas, perform rituals, or other methods. Do not exercise or practice yoga at all. No makeup is allowed. Wear simple, loose clothes. Respect other meditators, and avoid talking and making strong movements that affect the practitioner next to you, in the same room, or the general public. Do not use pen and paper to take notes during these ten days. Do not bring drinking water into the meditation room. In meditation rooms and Dhamma discourse rooms, there are only cushions. Those with leg pain are allowed to sit on chairs to meditate.

The meditation center has many separate buildings and meditation halls. This December 2023 course will have 100 men (including two Tibetan and Vietnamese monks) and 100 women (including thirty Vietnamese nuns) attending. Men and women live separately, eat separately, listen to Dhamma and meditate separately. Each room is shared by two people. There is a meditation teacher to guide each session. The organizers rarely hold the microphone to make noisy announcements. The program was posted on the board, and when it was time for the bell to shake gently, the practitioners natually gather according to the schedule and sit on cushions labeled with their names.

The bedroom has blankets, mosquito nets, and pillows. Students can only bring their pillowcases and bed sheets. Hot water is only turned on during breaks so students can bathe and wash. There is a yard with ropes to dry clothes. There is a dining room. After eating, practitioners can wash their plates and spoons. Nuns are assigned fixed tables to sit facing the wall and can come in to get food fifteen minutes before the laypeople to avoid waiting and crowding. Indian foods such as white rice, fried rice, chapati, papad, dal, gulab jamun, masala, mashed potatoes, boiled beets, and sweet potatoes were served accompanied by nutritious milk, tea, cakes, and fruits.

The organizers only serve breakfast and the noontime meal. After noon, old monastic meditators and old lay meditators are not allowed to eat. New monastics can drink sugared lemon juice, while lay practitioners can only drink milk tea. Students should not eat two or three plates at lunchtime to make up for no evening meal. Eat only until you are three-fourths full, just enough, not too full to meditate. Do not fast or be absent. All meditators must go down to the dining hall (eating a little is ok), because the organizers will worry if students are absent. Please be mindful of the organizers who are watching out for you.

Hot water for bathing and washing will be available during breaks: morning 7–8 a.m., noon 1–2 p.m., and afternoon 5–6 p.m. There is one hot tap and one cold tap. Open two faucets at the same time and you can shower and wash. There is a spacious drying yard in front of the room.

Monastic practitioners are highly respected. We are allowed to sit on chairs when presenting the Dhamma to the meditation master, and we are allowed to sit in the front row; we can get food and eat meals fifteen minutes before the public arrives. Monastic meditators are a model for lay practitioners to follow. Therefore, when walking, standing, sitting, lying down, eating, and drinking, the nuns keep gentle silence, are mindful and alert to all actions, and often come early to meditation sessions. Each group of about five people presents the Dhamma to the Master once a day. There is no need to report the sore feet, a runny nose, or the outside environment of chirping birds, noisy vehicles, blaring radio stations, and creaking doors. Only report to the Dhamma Master: the mind based on the breath, the breath in and out, and feel what state the breath touches: hot, cold, clear, hissing ... At noon from 12 to 12:30 p.m. and at night from 9:00 to 9:30 p.m., the practitioners can raise any question, and the teacher will answer.

Bodh Gaya Meditation Centre regularly organizes two ten-day meditation courses each month. There are new and old students. The old students attend regularly every year and after the Dhamma presentation, the teacher gives them permission to join the step-by-step ten-day meditation course, the eight-day sati courses, twenty-day, forty-five-day, and even sixty-day courses. If practitioners want to attend a long course, they must present the Dhamma and meet the required conditions. For example, the practitioners must attend ten of the ten-day courses and two of the sati eight-day courses within two years. Only then, can they proceed to the twenty-day course and must pass an interview with a master. In Sri Lanka, there are currently twenty-day retreats and multi-day retreats, while the ten-day retreats are only available in India, Vietnam, the United States, Canada, and many other countries. Former students are given IDs and passwords to enter the website[7] (by the organizers) to refer to the conditions for participating in long-term courses.

After participating in the meditation course, old students can register and volunteer to serve on the organization committee called Dhamma Server. Monks and nuns serve the group of bhikkhus and bhikṣuṇīs while laywomen serve women, and men serve men.

---

7   . https://os.vridhamma.org/node/350

There are many chores for the Dhamma servers such as ringing bells, distributing food, posting notices, reminding students, and solving needs during the course.

Mrs. Smt. Anupama Vinayak Jagtap is a female meditation master (about sixty years old) from Pune, India, guiding 100 female meditation students in Indian and English for this vipassana meditation course of December 15–26, 2023. The meditation master is a slim, gentle figure with a relaxed demeanor, and always smiles at the students.

*Meditation Master A. V. Jagtap (standing center),
Bhikṣuṇīs TN Giới Hương (next right) and Vietnamese
nun meditators*

In the ten-day schedule, practitioners must meditate every day from eight to eleven hours (4:00 a.m. to 9:30 p.m). There is also a Dhamma presentation once with the meditation master, the evening Dhamma discourse once for one hour (listening to a tape), and listening to the chanting in Hindi and English from the tape for fifteen minutes in the dawn, morning, afternoon, and evening. The late Master Goenka's chanting voice is warm, melodious, and joyful. These chants were compiled into the book, *The Gem Set in Gold* (A manual of pariyatti containing Pali and Hindi Chanting from a ten-day course of vipassana meditation as taught by Acharya S.N. Goenka, Vipassana Research Institute).

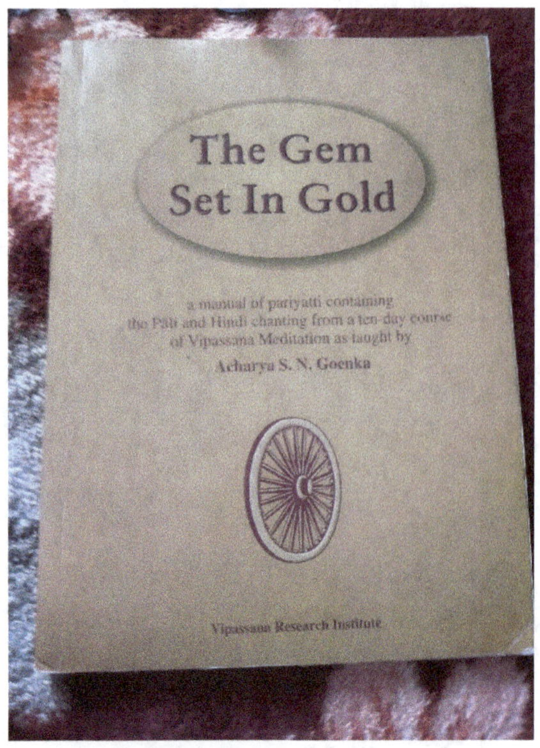

The Gem Set in Gold

Daily chanting for the ten-day vipassana course

5. CHANTING SUTTAS

Every day, practitioners often listen to the tape with the warm chanting voice of Master Goenka on the awakening, expressing gratitude to the three jewels (Buddha, Dharma, Sangha), teachers, parents, and returning merit[8] as follows:

AWAKE

People of the world, awake!

The dark night is over

The light of Dhamma has come

The dawn of happiness.

Come, beings of the universe

Listen to the wisdom of the Dhamma

In this lies happiness and peace

Freedom, liberation, nibbana.[9]

FIVE PRECEPTS

The five precepts (Sanskrit: pañcaśīla; Pali: pañcasīla) or five rules of training (Sanskrit: pañcaśikṣapada; Pali: pañcasikkhapada) are the most important system of morality for Buddhist laypeople.

---

8. *The Gem Set in Gold* – A manual of pariyatti containing Pali and Hindi chanting from a ten-day course of vipassana meditation as taught by Acharya S.N. Goenka. Vipassana Research Institute. 2009.

They constitute the basic code of ethics to be respected by lay followers of Buddhism. The precepts are commitments to abstain from killing living beings, stealing, sexual misconduct, lying, and intoxication.

Within the Buddhist doctrine, these precepts are meant to develop mind and character to make progress on the path of precept-concentration-wisdom and enlightenment.

RESPECT FOR TEACHERS

I pay homage to my revered teacher

Bowing my head at his feet

He gave me such a jewel of Dhamma

That evil cannot approach.

He let me taste Dhamma's nectar

Now no sensual pleasure can allure

Such an essence of Dhamma he gave

That the shell (of ignorance) dropped away.

REFUGE AT THE TRIPLE GEM

Those peaceful ones of peaceful mind

Whose refuge is the Triple Gem

In this world or beyond

Devas dwelling on earth or elsewhere.

Who are unceasingly acquiring numerous merits

May those devas come

Who dwell on royal Meru

The glorious golden mountains . . .

RETURNING MERIT

By the merits of this service

May Dhamma spread

May the darkness of evil be eradicated

May all beings be happy and prosperous.

May all beings be happy

May every tree, every blade of grass

And every particle of this earth

Be suffused with Dhamma

May all who meditate on this Dhamma land.

Be liberated from all suffering.

May all be happy!

May you be happy!

May all beings be happy!

The chanting voice is warm and slow, like Master Goenka's heavenly voice, full of energy from the power that meditation exudes. Hundreds of practitioners sit quietly cross-legged like statues, wholeheartedly listening to the chants in Hindi and English that pour drop by drop into our minds and spread throughout our bodies.

6. DHAMMA DISCOURSES

Every evening from 7–8 o'clock is the time to listen to the discourse (taped evening discourse). Three rooms serve three languages: Hindi, English, and Vietnamese. Each student goes to his/her language room. The content of the discourses in Vietnamese is as follows:

6.1. DISCOURSE ON THE FIRST DAY, DECEMBER 16, 2023:

Master Goenka teaches about keeping the five precepts (sila), especially the precept of avoiding wrong speech (lying, cruel words, double-tongued words). If we do not want to be deceived or cursed by others, we should not deceive or curse others to make them suffer.

Precepts are important because they lead to right concentration. Some people claim that vipassana meditation involves sitting still and doing nothing, so to keep the precepts is unnecessary. This understanding is wrong because only precepts lead to right concentration. Without precepts, meditators will let loose and violate the precepts. How can they sit still and practice?

Practitioners need to keep being aware of listening-thinking while meditating.

Listening: For example, seeing/listening to the food menu induces saliva naturally.

Thinking: Seeing people around eat delicious food, thinking that the food will be delicious, saliva flows naturally.

Practicing: Order food, eat it, and find it delicious.

Likewise, hearing an introduction to peaceful vipassana meditation is listening.

Seeing the meditation masters and meditators walking, standing, lying, and sitting in a dignified manner, gentle and charismatic, the practitioner immediately thinks that meditation must be beneficial.

Enroll in a ten-day meditation course and experience it for the real benefits.

The unconscious mind is the highest mind. The deep unconscious mind is sensitive and knows everything, just like one who has obtained enlightenment, he/she can see the truth. If we have not yet been enlightened, it will be easy to speak falsely. There is a story about two friends. A blind friend named A asked friend B: "What is the white color? Please describe it to me."

Friend B answers: "White is different from black."

Friend A: "But I'm blind. I don't know the black color."

Friend B saw the white goose in front of his eyes, so he quickly hugged it and showed it to

Friend A: "This is white."

Friend A touched the goose's feathers and uttered:

"Oh, I see, so white is soft."

When touching the duck's feet, he uttered:

"I know, white is like a fan."

He guesses all the time, but is still wrong. This shows that if there is blindness, the predictions will be all wrong. Likewise, if one has not yet been enlightened, he/she does not see the real truth.

6.2. DISCOURSE ON THE SECOND DAY, DECEMBER 17, 2023

Master Goenka defines Dhamma as neither a philosophy, nor an intellectual game, nor a devotional game but a practice, an experience.

Practice: Focus the breath right in the triangle of your nostrils, then observe the breath and experience the feeling of touching the breath, such as hot, cold, short, long, hissing breath. The more we feel its meticulous, detailed breathing up and down, the more alert, sharp, and delicate the sensitivity will become.

New practitioners will have back pain and aches when sitting, especially if they have to sit for eight to eleven hours a day, but if they work hard and be patient, their bodies will get used to sitting and they will feel comfortable. Meditating for ten days is like having a serious illness and going to see a doctor to have surgery. The patient will feel pain and discomfort, but when the illness is gone, he/she will feel comfortable. Like a finger pricked by a tree chip. If we don't take it out, we will feel uncomfortable and when we take it out, it will be extremely painful, but we will be healthy and light.

6.3. DISCOURSE ON THE THIRD DAY, DECEMBER 18, 2023

Master Goenka taught the Four Noble Truths consisting of suffering, the origin of suffering, the cessation of suffering, and the path of cessation of suffering.

Contemplate that this body is a combination of countless microscopic cells. There is no enduring "self." The Four Foundations of Mindfulness Sutta is called contemplation of the body on the body.

The person I am today is different from the person I was yesterday. The river passing by in the afternoon will be different from the river now. There is no self or ego, just countless microscopic particles of tiny water drops combined to be something we call a river.

Vipassana helps us understand this: contemplating the body on the body. Less body movement: if there is movement, the practitioner observes the movement through feeling/sense and scans from head to toe: face, neck, right shoulder, left shoulder, armrest, palm, fingers, abdomen, thighs, and legs feeling itchy, hot, cold, painful, or uncomfortable. Know clearly, like a scanner seeing each passing object.

The gross mind will not receive the sensations in this biochemical, biological body. A focused and subtle mind will receive the sutble sensations such as sweating, pulse jumping, heart beating, blood flowing, and clothes touching the skin. When there is pain and discomfort, when the dislike or boredom arise, realize this is just a habit. When everything is comfortable and soft then you love it. It clearly shows that feelings and sensations are impermanent, arising and passing away, changing. When we know this, if we don't cling tightly suffering from attachment will stop.

Master Goenka teaches that until the third day of meditation if the practitioners cannot feel the breath, we should hold our breath for one or two minutes. Indeed, in just half a minute, we will immediately feel hot or cold breath right in our nostrils. Due to holding the breath, discomfort and lack of air, we get more focus on seeing the breath, the life present now at the nostril, and then we concentrate on observing.

6.4. DISCOURSE ON THE FOURTH DAY, DECEMBER 19, 2023

The last three days were focused on exercising morality (sila) and concentration (samadhi) to prepare for today, the fourth day of wisdom (meditation). Today is truly practicing vipassana.

1–1:45 p.m. meditate

1:45–2 p.m. rest

3:00 p.m. Vipassana instruction begins

The sign on the meditation hall in Vietnamese: "Hãy cố gắng đúng giờ và an vui tu tập. Hãy an vui." ("Try to be on time and practice happily. Be happy.")

Practice: The mind only focuses on the triangle right at the nostril, feeling and sensing right at the nostril, the breath on the left, right, or both sides. We are instructed to not mix this practice with yoga or other breathing meditation methods because it will be harmful and ineffective. Practice mastering our distracting habits. If we observe carefully, we will see all the sensations: pleasant sensations will give rise to liking. The uncomfortable feeling when sitting with numb legs is uncomfortable, so contemplate impermanence so as not to cling to it. Just a feeling of leg pain, coming and going, not real. Seeing the discomfort as comfortable, we will get used to it over time. Teach our body (it's comfortable, not uncomfortable because of leg pain) that discomfort and comfort are the same manner of changing sensations. Foot pain is like the habit of hating bad food and liking good food; we are used to this flow. Now, the practitioners are training the body and mind not to like it or hate it—just observe. Letting go is easy when we realize this idea. Overcoming the feeling of numb legs during meditation is a big challenge for new meditators.

There is a story that once the Buddha taught vipassana in Sravasti when a young man came and asked: "Blessed One, you are a great man. Why don't you save all sentient beings quickly since you have compassion for all species?" The Buddha replied that his love was to bring the vipassana method to each person to practice and save themselves. Relying on the medium of breathing to purify the mind is like a doctor prescribing medicine, but the patient must take it to save himself.

One day, Master Goenka (at that time a

businessperson) went to a medical clinic and met a doctor. He thought he would be waiting because usually there were many patients. However, when he arrived, he found there were no patients and no customers. Master Goenka asked the reason. The doctor replied: "So boring! At this time, there is no epidemic, so it is slower than last month; there are not many patients."

Back home, the businessman Goenka thought this doctor had no ethics, hoping a disease would spread as he would earn more if many people were sick. However, lost in thinking, he realized that businessmen like him and others were even more evil. For example, traders who hope for war will say that the economy will develop because scarce goods will be expensive, and trade will make a lot of profit. If it's peacetime, the economy is normal, goods are plentiful and prices are stable and businessmen don't make much money.

Then Master Goenka continued to teach the precepts, the Eightfold Path, and guided the meditators to focus on feeling the subtlety of the breath in the triangle of the nostrils. Moving to a higher level means not only observing the breath but also the feeling of hot and cold in the breath. There are small sensations in the breath in the nostrils; pay attention to any sensations arising. The more we see the little details, the better the mind becomes, and the more sensitive, intelligent, and awakened it becomes.

6.5. DISCOURSE ON THE FIFTH DAY, DECEMBER 20, 2023

Practice meditation in a cell or a private room.

The meditation center has an area consisting of small, narrow rows of rooms next to each other, built underground and called the basement. Each row has about twenty-five rooms facing each other. Each room is two meters long x one meter wide (small and narrow for easily concentrating the mind), so it is called a cell (like a small cell in a prison or a closed retreat). There was nothing in the room, except for a cushion on the ground to sit on, a lamp, and a opening in the ceiling to let air in. On the floor, there are square tiles (each about 0.5 meters long) and the ceiling is covered with a small, beautiful blue corrugated iron roof. Those practitioners who feel uncomfortable sitting in these narrow cells can ask permission to meditate in the meditation hall or their room.

Practicing meditation in a crowded meditation hall can easily distract the mind, while a small cell or a separate cell will help the practitioners go deeper into meditation.

On the board is written: "Today sit with strong adhithana determination," meaning that today is the middle of the course, so please practice minimizing moving and changing positions. For example, at first the practitioner changes positions four or five times. Today, only one or two times or not moving at all. So determined!

The meditation center recommends sitting three times without changing position (adhithana) which are 8–9 a.m., 2:30–3:30 p.m., and 6–7 p.m. Let's practice happily.

6.6. DISCOURSE ON THE SIXTH DAY, DECEMBER 21, 2023

A businessman enrolled in the ten-day vipassana course gave the comment that "The lecture hall, meditation hall, room, discourse hall, landscape, dining room, food, and organization are very wonderful, except the meditation. My feet hurt so much. Every day, I sit for eight to eleven hours, which is too much, causing my limbs to ache."

The meditation master teaches: "Look directly at the foot pain, the uncomfortable feeling, go beyond the foot pain, you will see that it is just the feeling of foot pain . . . it will change, quickly, fleeting, impermanent, it is not real, then you won't be ordered (by your leg) to move and change positions to be comfortable."

The story of saving a father: There was a young man who was sad and crying because his father had died. He came to ask the Buddha to save his father. He begged the Buddha: "I think that ordinary monks can perform rituals to save the dead, enter a new country, or have a 'green card' to stay. What's more, the Buddha is an enlightened, liberated, great man. Please, have mercy and give my father a green card to stay in a peaceful world."

Buddha taught: "You have two pots: one contains pebbles and one has avocados, and you throw them both into the river." The young man was so happy because he thought Buddha was finding a way to save his father. The bucket containing the pebbles sinks to the bottom of the river, while the bucket containing the avocados floats on the river's surface. The Buddha asked the young man to invite monks to chant suttas until pebbles and stones float to the surface of the river.

The young man quickly replied: "Blessed One, it can never be possible because the rocks are heavy and must sink."

The Buddha explained that in the same way, if his father created bad karma while alive, he would sink and not be able to rise by reciting the sutta. The son understands and accepts the doctrine of impermanence and karma.

The story of clinging to "self": A poor old woman was given a train ticket to attend a vipassana meditation retreat for ten days. She had twenty rupees (equivalent to a U.S. dollar at that time), a silver bracelet worth twenty rupees (dowry) and a piece of candy. When she meditates, eats, and takes a shower, wherever she goes, she keeps her bag next to her.

One day, she cried bitterly. When asked the reason, it turned out that her bag containing silver bracelets and money had been lost. She refused to meditate any more and kept crying because she loved that twenty-rupee bracelet very much. Everyone collected money and gave her 100 rupees even though her bag was only worth forty rupees, but she still cried because she missed the precious bracelet . . . and firmly believed she had to find it for herself. Luckily, a gardener later saw a monkey eating candy and holding her bag. He chased it and got her bag back. The old woman was happy. She stopped crying and became happy again. It's all due to the strong attachment. So when meditating, don't bring valuables with you, and if you do, keep them in a locked cabinet of the organizers, and you keep the key.

6.7. DISCOURSE ON THE SEVENTH DAY, DECEMBER 22, 2023

On the sign at the door of the meditation hall is written: "Continuous practice is the key to success."

Today, students should practice reflecting on the body: up and down, up and down, down and up, whole or in part, meditate from feet to thighs, thighs to abdomen, abdomen to chest, chest to forehead, forehead to head, and vice versa from top to bottom.

Be aware of the sensations in every movement and thought—picking up food and walking back and forth, the feeling of picking up food and walking back and forth.

When we feel sleepy, open our eyes and look down; hold our earlobes and pull them down to wake up.

Today's discourse teaches about suffering: Depending on each person's perception, suffering can be pessimistic or optimistic. For example, a mother gave her son ten rupees to buy cooking oil. After buying it, the boy accidentally tripped and fell, spilled half the bottle, and went home crying in fear because of the oil spillage. That is a pessimistic attitude.

The mother again gave ten rupees to her older son to buy oil. Halfway there, the boy also fell and spilled half of the oil. Returning home, the child happily said: "Mom, I fell, and luckily I caught it, so there's half of the oil left, only half of it was poured out." This is an optimistic attitude.

Thus, it is spilled oil but there are pessimists and optimists. So happiness and suffering are not real, just a fleeting feeling of each person's delusion.

Later, when practicing meditation to improve, there will be twenty, thirty, forty-five, and sixty-day retreats, without five minutes of rest or as many breaks as in the first ten-day course.

6.8. DISCOURSE ON THE EIGHTH DAY, DECEMBER 23, 2023

On the board is written: "Awake every moment."

"Keep your mind balanced every moment."

The lecture focuses on diligence, awareness, mindfulness, being sensitive to feelings, and keeping a balanced mind.

The story of how the pagans sought to defeat the Buddha: Some religious scholars liked to argue and challenge the Buddha, but the Buddha always answered calmly and with great wisdom. Therefore, it was very difficult to defeat him.

In their discussion, they considered that if they were to approach the Buddha with inquiries about practices involving animal skins, ashes, kneeling on one knee, or consuming only a sesame seed a day—methods aimed at unsettling the Buddha—he would likely refrain from responding, as he did not involve himself with such conduct.

The Buddha only taught morality, concentration, and wisdom. Engaging in this practice allows Buddhists to personally witness the accuracy of his statements, making it impossible to dispute the Buddha's teachings. The pagan group thought everyone likes money and women, so what about the Buddha? About money: He was not interested in riches because he was Crown Prince Siddhartha. After witnessing sickness, death, and old age, he left his palace and wealth in pursuit of a spiritual path to understand the nature of existence.

About women: Everyone likes beautiful women. One evening, a beautiful woman emerged from the direction of the Buddha's retreat with her hair flowing, clothes in disarray, and exclaimed loudly, "I had an amazing night with Shakyamuni Buddha." The people around thought she was crazy, so they didn't pay any attention to her. Eight months later, the beautiful girl came with a big pregnant belly (padded with a pillow on her belly) to the lecture hall, where the Buddha was teaching with a large number of kings and laypeople. She shouted: "Hey Buddha, what are you going to do with this fetus?"

The Buddha felt compassion and pity for this woman, a victim of the pagan group; he did not feel anger or hatred. Had he succumbed to anger, he could have instructed the king and officials who were listening to behead the girl according to the law. The Buddha's compassionate force radiated; the young woman transformed and felt confused. At that moment, a mouse ran up and bit the rope around her abdomen, dropping the fake fetus.

The Buddha always had a heart of understanding and compassion. People who practice vipassana always develop compassion. For example, there was a robber who abused a young girl. If a vipassana meditator harbors love for the victim, a young girl, his compassion for the robber will be doubly strong. Recognizing the criminal's descent into sin, the meditator should use his influence to reach out and rescue the wrongdoer out of pity. This mirrors the tale of the bandit Angulimala, who severed the fingers of ninety-nine victims, illustrating a similar theme.

6.9. DISCOURSE ON THE NINTH DAY, DECEMBER 24, 2023

Anger, craving, and foolishness are abstract biochemical reactions. They are more difficult to see than focusing on the breath, a specific object. Vipassana helps us see anger and its fleeting nature of impermanence.

We cannot change the world, but we can change ourselves through vipassana.

There is a story about an artist who painted a picture of a beautiful woman, only to find himself in love with the image. He tried to find her to be his wife and not being able to find the woman, he experienced deep sorrow. Then, the artist drew an ugly devil. He became terrified and ran away, haunted by his own creation. This narrative underscores the idea that both beautiful and malevolent figures are crafted by artists. Emotions and perceptions, similarly, are self-generated and inherently artificial.

There is a story of a queen and king meditating together. When both finished meditating, they begin to question each other.

The queen asked: "Your Majesty, who do you love most in the world?"

The king replied: "I love myself the most."

The king asked: "Who do you love the most in the world?"

The queen replied: "I love myself the most in the world."

Both answered correctly in the spirit of vipassana because if someone loves, pampers, and serves us, then we love that person, so this is self-cherishing.

Practitioners who practice vipassana for ten days keep the five precepts and ten paramitas for ten days. The ten paramitas (pāramī) are as follows:

1. The perfection of giving (dāna pāramī)

2. The perfection of morality (sīla pāramī)

3. The perfection of renunciation (nekkhamma pāramī)

4. The perfection of wisdom (paññā pāramī)

5. The perfection of diligence (viriya pāramī)

6. The perfection of patience (khanti pāramī)

7. The perfection of truth (sacca pāramī)

8. The perfection of aspiration (adhitthāna pāramī)

9. The perfection of loving-kindness (mettā pāramī)

10. The perfection of equanimity (upekkha pāramī)

Among the ten paramitas, the eighth perfection is the resolute vow power, and the sixth paramita is patience and endurance. The resolution—even though our legs are numb, our back hurts, we still don't move or open our eyes; we sit still like a statue. At the Niranjara River, under the Bodhi tree, the Buddha vowed that if he had not yet been enlightened, he would meditate quietly, not moving or standing up. If his prayer comes true, he would let his alms bowl float upstream. Indeed, he dropped his alms bowl on the surface of the Niranjana River; his alms bowl floated upstream to demonstrate paramita's resolute vow.

Master Goenka tells the story of the early days of establishing the vipassana meditation center. He told the board of directors the organization should offer retreats freely, without charging for food, rooms, and not charging for lectures. He explained that if you take money for food, the meditators will ask for this or that dish and think "I paid money, I would like this or that dish." The same goes for the room and teaching style. Now, without taking money, the organizers can cook whatever they want and assign whatever room they think is suitable, Practitioners are more likely to be satisfied if there is no set required fee. Like monks, they partake of whatever food is offered to them, recognizing it as the gift of life.

The board of directors was worried that if they didn't charge a fee, there would be a lot of poor people coming in and the retreat center would not survive. Master

Goenka replied: "If individuals come in to eat and reside, they will meditate from eight to eleven hours a day, from 4 a.m. to 9 p.m. If they can meditate like that, they are eligible to receive food and lodging."

Today, the ninth day of the course, is the last day of noble silence. Tomorrow is the final day, the tenth day. At noon tomorrow, practitioners will be able to pick up their cell phones and other belongings and be able to talk to people around them.

6.10. DISCOURSE ON THE TENTH DAY, DECEMBER 25, 2023

Today, the tenth day of practicing metta, we watched the movie, *Doing Time, Doing Vipassana,* in which the prisoners practice vipassana meditation and listen to the life of the late Master Goenka.

METTA BHAVANA

9 a.m. Meditate together

9–10 a.m. Guided meditation

(End of holy silence and we are encouraged to remember to maintain silence in and around the meditation hall.)

2:30–3:45 p.m. Meditate together and practice metta

6–7 p.m. Meditate together

7–8 p.m. Discourse (no meditation after the discourse)

At noon, before mealtime, the students can take out their phones and belongings and talk on the phone or with people around them. This is also the time to make offerings to the Dhamma Bodhi Meditation Centre. Practitioners undergo ten days of peace and on the last day, they are allowed to make offerings. The center is maintained thanks to the joyful offerings of each practitioner, so almost everyone registers to make offerings and receives a receipt of donation.

At 1:00 p.m., we watch the movie. *Doing Time, Doing Vipassana,*[10] directed by Aylet Menahemi and Eilona Ariel, produced by the Vipassana Research Institute, India's Karuna Films in 1997. The movie is fifty-two minutes long. This award-winning documentary takes the practitioners into India's largest prison, one of the strictest in the world. It shows the dramatic changes brought by bringing vipassana meditation into the prison.

We hear the story of a strong woman named Kiran Bedi, a former Inspector General of Prisons in New Delhi. She tried to turn the infamous Tihar Jail, once a hellhole of crime, into an oasis of peace and well-being It is a story about the ancient meditation method of Sakyamuni Buddha, vipassana, taught by the Myanmar meditation master, Āchariya S.N. Goenka. It helped every prisoner, regardless of skin color or religion, take control of their lives and work for the benefit of themselves and others. Above all, it is the story of prisoners who undergo profound spiritual change and realize that incarceration is not the end, but it can be the beginning of a new life, if only the prisoner knows to practice vipassana meditation.

---

10. https://en.wikipedia.org/wiki/Doing_Time,_Doing_Vipassana

METTA SUTTA MEDITATION is a way to nurture and spread understanding and love to all living beings so that all can transform suffering, be peaceful and liberated as the Metta Sutta[11] teaches:

May everyone and all species live in safety and happiness, with gentle and carefree thoughts.

May all creatures on earth live peacefully—the weak, the strong, the tall, the short, the big, the small, the ones we can see, the species that we cannot see, near species, species that are far away, species that have been born and species that are about to be born.

Pray that no one will kill any other, no one should underestimate anyone else's life, no one out of anger or malice will wish for anyone to suffer and be miserable.

The work of nine days of meditation: Cleaning the grass of negative afflictions with mindfulness.

On the last day: Sow the seeds of compassion for suffering sentient beings in the fertile soil of a pure mind as exemplified by the late Master S.N. Goenka's dedication:

"May all suffering people of the world understand Dhamma, may they practice Dhamma, may they apply Dhamma in their day-to-day life, and come out of all the agonies of a defiled mind full of negativities. May all enjoy the peace and harmony of a pure mind, a mind full of compassionate love and goodwill towards other beings."[12]

---

11. Metta Sutta, Sutta Nipata I, Thích Nhất Hạnh dịch.
12. https://os.vridhamma.org/Old-Students

THE LIFE OF MEDITATION MASTER GOENKA

Today is the last day; students can listen to the story of the life of Myanmar meditation master, Āchariya Goenka. He was originally a rich businessman in Myanmar. He was very successful in trade and industry, so he was quite wealthy. However, he suffered from chronic headaches and spent a lot of money trying to find a cure, but no one could help with this disease. The doctor had to inject opium to relieve his pain. Injecting opium has side effects of addiction and withdrawal. Then, the doctor advised him to travel for a few months to forget about business and illness.

Master Goenka went to Switzerland, the Netherlands, Italy, and Japan for several months. Doctors in these countries also treated him for the headaches where he spent lots of time and money, but nothing helped. A Myanmar friend advised him to practice meditation for ten days under the guidance of Myanmar Master Sayagyi U Ba Khin.

Master Sayagyi U Ba Khin met Goenka and said that Goenka still kept his family's Indian Hindu practices and was not affected by vipassana meditation. However, he was encouraged not to bow to the Buddha or practice god-worshipping rituals during these ten days. Despite Goenka's reluctance, rooted in his deep respect for the Buddha and his habitual worship and prostration practices, Master Sayagyi U Ba Khin insisted he abstain from such rituals. Goenka expressed his intention to practice vipassana to alleviate his illness, but the Master clarified that vipassana is not intended as a medical treatment, rather, its purpose is to purify the mind. Despite initial resistance, Goenka joined the retreat but considered quitting after just two days. A foreign teacher observed this and encouraged him to stay for an additional one or two days, as the results of vipassana typically manifest on the third or fourth day.

He endured it one more day. Indeed, the peace and concerntration came and lasted the rest of his life. Goenka was very grateful to that teacher. His headaches were gone and his mind was peaceful.

Goenka's parents were sick in Myanmar and had to go to India for treatment. He wanted to share this vipassana meditation method with his parents, so he went to India and began teaching meditation to his parents and relatives. From a few dozen people attending meditation at first, it increased to hundreds, thousands, including Hindus, Muslims, Buddhists, Christians, politicians, social leaders, intellectuals, and common people—all came to learn the Buddha's vipassana meditation method. At first, he taught one course, two courses, and later thousands of courses.

6.11. MORNING OF THE ELEVENTH DAY, DECEMBER 26, 2023

In the group of Vietnamese Buddhist nuns, some have attended more than ten courses, or several courses and for some this is first course. Former monastics registered to volunteer to help Vietnamese monks and nuns, such as Bhikṣuṇī Chúc Hân (Xuan Thanh Pagoda, Dong Nai Province) and Bhikṣuṇī Minh Nhu (Vien

Khong Nunnery, Ba Ria, Vung Tau Province) for the previous ten days. They were on the Dhamma Servers team to translate and help other nun practitioners according to the rules of the vipassana center.

A group of Vietnamese nuns held a gratitude ceremony for the female master, Smt. Anupama Vinayak Jagtap. We sent some gifts of Vietnamese cakes to this Master who has steadfastly guided us and others over the past ten days.

Bhikṣuṇī TN Gioi Huong and the nuns thanked Master Smt. Anupama Vinayak Jagtap

Discussing feedback after completing the ten-day meditation course, Bhikṣuṇī Pháp Huệ (a student at Andhra University, Visakhapatnam, Andhra Pradesh, India) shared:

Through the meditation course, I have experienced and learned something important to do in life. The world and all phenomena are impermanent, but in impermanence, we can learn vipassana, an art of living, to bring happiness and peace for ourselves and many. Vipassana will help more and more people know the Dhamma and know how to overcome the feeling of suffering in this life.

Bhikṣuṇī Tịnh Hỷ (a student at Andhra University, Visakhapatnam, Andhra Pradesh, India) revealed her thoughts:

Since the moment I opened my eyes until now, I have been entangled in the pursuit of desires, grappling with anger, and navigating through delusion. Since participating in the first vipassana meditation course (2022) and the second time (2023) at Master Goenka's meditation center in India, I have been like a person in the dark who has found light. Observing the feeling of contemplation on the body helps me gradually realize that feelings are impermanent and that reactions only increase suffering, so the frequency of being influenced, although present, has decreased. The evening discourses, stories of Master Goenka's experiences, and simply explanations help us understand more deeply the teachings of Dependent Origination and the Five Aggregates. Listening to the discourse without taking notes, every word he taught was like medicine to help me develop more faith and love for the Buddha.

CHAPTER 3

CONCLUSION

Vipassana meditation is the experience of gradual reflection and gradual liberation that naturally comes due to diligence, awareness, mindfulness, and the dedicated practice of each meditator. The key to meditation is observation and seeing clearly, called insight, which will help balance emotions, reduce negativity and stress, and increase clarity and peace.

Attending a ten-day vipassana course is to let the body rest because it has worked hard all its life, and these ten days are dedicated to turning inward through meditation, free from the distractions of email, cell phones, Facebook, virtual TikTok, or other forms of chaotic communication.

Instead, we focus only on breathing, contemplating the body, contemplating feelings, and increasing positive life energy.

The Dhamma Bodhi Meditation Centre retreats are held regularly every half month (in Bodh Gaya, India, and many other places). These are completely free and offered on a dana basis. The masters do not receive any financial or material remuneration. Rooms, food, electricity, and water are completely free. Where are the funds? All financial support comes from the contributions of old students who have attended previous courses, enjoyed the benefits of vipassana and want to give others, especially those new to vipassana, the opportunity to enjoy the mental, as well as spiritual, benefits as we have. What a noble and highly effective way of teaching the Dhamma!

Vipassana has specific practical benefits in the present and future. Therefore, there are many laypeople of different religions from many countries who dedicate themselves to work, trade, and make a lot of money to act as the Dhamma protectors and Dhamma servers, specializing in making offerings and building new centers and providing free volunteer service to many meditation centers. The participating practitioners saw the benefits for their bodies and minds, so they continuously registered to attend many courses. Consequently, the late Master Goenkaji's vipassana meditation centers flourished and gained increasing popularity.

The meditation course is finished. All practitioners

carry their luggages and step out of the meditation hall, returning to their busy, daily life of the six senses facing the six worlds, but for many meditators, it seems like something has happened to change their minds. They anticipate that life will become more meaningful with vipassana.

Winter 2023 in Bodhgaya, India

With Metta,

Ven. Dr. Bhikṣuṇī TN Giới Hương

Huongsentemple@gmail.com

*From left: Bhikṣuṇī Vien Nhuan, Bhikṣuṇī Tinh Hy,
Dr. Bhikṣuṇī TN Gioi Huong, Bhikṣuṇī Phap Hue
and a Bhikṣuṇī in front of the gate of Dhamma Bodhi
Meditation Centre*

SOURCES

1. Bodh Gaya International Vipassana Meditation Centre, Bodhgaya, Bihar, India, Trung tâm Thiền Tứ Niệm Xứ Quốc tế Bodhgaya, Bồ Đề Đạo Tràng, bang Bihar, Ấn Độ, accessed 1/19/24., https://bodhi.dhamma.org/.

2. Goenka, Acharya S. N. , *The Gem Set in Gold* (A manual of pariyatti containing Pali and Hindi chanting from a ten-day course of vipassana meditation as taught by Acharya S.N. Goenka). Vipassana Research Institute. 2009. Trang 7–15; Trang 5.

3. Hanh, Nhất Thich, Metta Sutta, Sutta Nipata I, accessed 1/22/24, https://www.youtube.com/watch?v=H2PRPdqQzGk

4. Insight Meditation Society, Barre, Massachusetts, USA, accessed 1/22/24, https://www.dhamma.org.

5. Kinh Tứ Niệm Xứ. Hải Triều Âm, accessed 1/22/24, https://chuaduocsu.org/tu-niem-xu/ *and* https://daibaothapmandalataythien.org/kinh-tu-niem-xu-tkn-hai-trieu-am

6. Menahemi, Ayelet and Eilona, Ariet T., *Doing Time, Doing Vipassana*, accessed 1/22/24, https://en.wikipedia.org/wiki/Doing_Time,_Doing_Vipassana.

7. Nanamoli, Bhikkhu and Bhikkhu Bodhi, The Middle Length Discourses of the Buddha, A Translation of the Majjhima Nikāya, Boston: Wisdom Publications, 2001.

8. Thiền Vipassana, (Directory) accessed 1/19/24, https://www.dhamma.org/vi/locations/directory#002.

9. Vipassana Research Institute (Old Students' Website, phải là thiền sinh cũ, được Ban tổ chức đưa ID và mật mã mới vào được website để lấy thông tin). Accessed 1/19/24. https://os.vridhamma.org/Old-Students.

APPENDIX 1

TEACHINGS OF THE SATIPAṬṬHĀNA SUTTA THE FOUR FOUNDATIONS OF MINDFULNESS

Compiled by Master Bhikṣuṇī Hai Trieu Am

Translation by Bhikṣuṇī TN Giới Hương

BOW HEAD AND TOUCH BOTH HANDS IN REVERENCE

- Pay homage to the Masters who have taught us to practice.

- Thank you to the Dharma friends who have helped us practice and study.

- We ask those with wisdom to teach and guide us.

- Please, may the Compassionate Ones guide us on the Dharma path.

- May all sentient beings in the ten directions achieve wisdom and liberation.

THE AWAKENING WORDS

(By Bhikkhu Sidhimuni, a graduate of Thailand's
National Pali College)

At Kuru, the Buddha taught the Four Foundations of Mindfulness. His delicate words are like pearls decorating a skillfully carved gold box.

The climate of Kuru is good and the plants have a lot of vitality. The people are strong, capable and interested in deep contemplation. They loved the Four Foundations of Mindfulness (Satipaṭṭhāna Sutta) so much that when the helpers washed clothes by the river or sat at a loom, they were only interested in discussing the Satipaṭṭhāna Sutta.

Anyone who does not practice the Four Foundations of Mindfulness will be blamed by the whole village for being a corpse that soils the ground. Whoever practices the Four Foundations of Mindfulness will immediately be praised: "How good! Life has human qualities."

The Four Foundations of Mindfulness is an unparalleled teaching that gives us a taste of Nirvana. There are two types of enlightenment: awakening and insight. Enlightenment means to receive what you inherently have. Observe to transform the delusion, ignorance, and any negatives that hinder enlightenment. The Four Foundations of Mindfulness reveals the wisdom of insight. It absorbs our four postures and appears in our three karmas of body, speech, and mind. Our mind must be a mirror that always shines. Thanks to insight, we can observe every thought, every action, every breath. Only then will we be able to purify the seeds of ignorance, habits from past lives.

Firstly, we must stay away from the attachments of the past and the future. We firmly believe that human life is completely dictated by our karma, and so as long as we transform the negative karma, we will enjoy peace and happiness. The right view is important because it leads to liberation. Eliminate all conscious calculations, focusing only on the present. When walking and standing, focus on posture; when sitting and lying down; focus on breathing. Over time, the coarse thoughts fade away, the outer world is no longer attached, and we see impermanence and selflessness. Life is only built on two fragile breaths, in and out.

The sutta teaches: "Breathe out, know how to breathe out; breathe in, know how to breathe in." Recently in Burma, Zen Master Mahasi taught that "When the belly is bulging, you know it's bulging; when the belly is flat, you know it's flat." It is intended to advise us that breathing through the abdomen and avoiding sympathetic nerve activity in the heart makes it easier for our mind to calm down. This way of breathing prevents strong emotions from arising. From a physiological standpoint, this is the key that closes the door tightly, preventing illusion from entering the mind.

Among the billions of humans, we are fortunate to have a human body that has the ability to hear the Buddha's Dharma. We must strive diligently to seek precept-concentration-wisdom. We hope that we will achieve enlightenment in this very life. If we miss this human opportunity, we will still be in the cycle of constant birth and death. We earnestly need to exchange this old, sick, and dead body for the real body of precept-meditation-wisdom.

Definitely! The worldly path of fame and fortune cannot lead to the right view. Buddhist disciples are determined to study the way to reach Nirvana.

PAY HOMAGE

1. From the hell, sinners can rise to their good mind.

   Namo Shakyamuni Buddha.

2. In the measureless kalpas, the result is full and the cause is round.

   Namo Shakyamuni Buddha.

3. One birth replenishes the land, in the Tusita heaven.

   Namo Shakyamuni Buddha.

4. Manifested a body, for the sake of many in the saha world.

   Namo Shakyamuni Buddha.

5. From the Tusita descends, fulfilling Ma Ya Queen's dream.

   Namo Shakyamuni Buddha.

6. Appeared in the royal palace and appeared reincarnated.

   Namo Shakyamuni Buddha.

7. Under the Ashoka tree, the Buddha is born.

Namo Shakyamuni Buddha.

8. Surrounded by desires, but detached from them.

Namo Shakyamuni Buddha.

9. Travel at four palace gates to see old age, illness, and death.

Namo Shakyamuni Buddha.

10. At midnight left the palace to be a wanderer who searched for the truth.

Namo Shakyamuni Buddha.

11. Cuts his hair at a remote mountain, finds the Teacher and the teachings.

Namo Shakyamuni Buddha.

12. At the snow Mountain, he practiced six years of asceticism.

Namo Shakyamuni Buddha.

13. Under the Bodhi tree, He subdued the demons.

Namo Shakyamuni Buddha.

14. As soon as the morning star rises, the path of enlightenment is complete. Namo Shakyamuni Buddha.

15. Forty-nine full years of preaching Dharma to save sentient beings.

Namo Shakyamuni Buddha.

16. The three vehicles are enough, the transformation has just been completed.

Namo Shakyamuni Buddha.

17. Under the two Sala trees, he manifested Nirvana.

Namo Shakyamuni Buddha.

18. Save the Buddha's relics, bring blessings to heaven and humans.

Namo Shakyamuni Buddha.

19. The Master of the Saha world is great and compassionate.

Namo Shakyamuni Buddha.

20. At the ashram, hundreds of billions of his incarnations.

Namo Shakyamuni Buddha.

***

SATIPAṬṬHĀNA SUTTA[13]
THE FOUR FOUNDATIONS OF MINDFULNESS

Translated from the Pali by Nyanasatta Thera

Thus have I heard. At one time the Blessed One was living among the Kurus, at Kammasadamma, a market town of the Kuru people. There the Blessed One addressed the bhikkhu thus: "Monks," and they replied to him, "Venerable Sir." The Blessed One spoke as follows:

---

13. Satipaṭṭhāna Sutta (The Four Foundations of Mindfulness), translated from the Pali by Nyanasatta Thera. Can be accessed at https://www.accesstoinsight.org/tipitaka/mn/mn.010.nysa.html.

This is the only way, monks, for the purification of beings, for the overcoming of sorrow and lamentation, for the destruction of suffering and grief, for reaching the right path, for the attainment of Nibbana, namely, the four foundations of mindfulness. What are the four?

Herein (in this teaching) a monk lives contemplating the body in the body, ardent, clearly comprehending and mindful, having overcome, in this world, covetousness and grief.

He lives contemplating feelings in feelings, ardent, clearly comprehending and mindful, having overcome, in this world, covetousness and grief.

He lives contemplating consciousness in consciousness, ardent, clearly comprehending and mindful, having overcome, in this world, covetousness and grief.

He lives contemplating mental objects in mental objects, ardent, clearly comprehending and mindful, having overcome, in this world, covetousness and grief.

I. CONTEMPLATION OF THE BODY

1.1. Mindfulness of Breathing

And how does a monk live contemplating the body in the body?

Herein, monks, a monk, having gone to the forest, to the foot of a tree or to an empty place, sits down with his legs crossed, keeps his body erect and his mindfulness alert.

Ever mindful he breathes in, mindful he breathes out. Breathing in a long breath, he knows, "I am breathing in a long breath"; breathing out a long breath, he knows, "I am breathing out a long breath"; breathing in a short breath, he knows, "I am breathing in a short breath"; breathing out a short breath, he knows, "I am breathing out a short breath."

"Experiencing the whole (breath-) body, I shall breathe in," thus he trains himself. "Experiencing the whole (breath-) body, I shall breathe out," thus he trains himself. "Calming the activity of the (breath-) body, I shall breathe in," thus he trains himself. "Calming the activity of the (breath-) body, I shall breathe out," thus he trains himself.

Just as a skillful turner or turner's apprentice, making a long turn, knows, "I am making a long turn," or making a short turn, knows, "I am making a short turn," just so the monk, breathing in a long breath, knows, "I am breathing in a long breath"; breathing out a long breath, he knows, "I am breathing out a long breath"; breathing in a short breath, he knows, "I am breathing in a short breath"; breathing out a short breath, he knows, "I am breathing out a short breath." "Experiencing the whole (breath-) body, I shall breathe in," thus he trains himself. "Experiencing the whole (breath-) body, I shall breathe out," thus he trains himself. "Calming the activity of the (breath-) body, I shall breathe in," thus he trains himself. "Calming the activity of the (breath-) body, I shall breathe out," thus he trains himself.

Thus he lives contemplating the body in the body

internally, or he lives contemplating the body in the body externally, or he lives contemplating the body in the body internally and externally. He lives contemplating origination factors in the body, or he lives contemplating dissolution factors in the body, or he lives contemplating origination-and-dissolution factors in the body. Or his mindfulness is established with the thought: "The body exists," to the extent necessary just for knowledge and mindfulness, and he lives detached, and clings to nothing in the world. Thus also, monks, a monk lives contemplating the body in the body.

1.2. Postures of the Body

And further, monks, a monk knows, when he is going, "I am going"; he knows, when he is standing, "I am standing"; he knows, when he is sitting, "I am sitting"; he knows, when he is lying down, "I am lying down"; or just as his body is disposed so he knows it.

Thus he lives contemplating the body in the body internally, or he lives contemplating the body in the body externally, or he lives contemplating the body in the body internally and externally. He lives contemplating origination factors in the body, or he lives contemplating dissolution factors in the body, or he lives contemplating origination-and-dissolution factors in the body. Or his mindfulness is established with the thought: "The body exists," to the extent necessary just for knowledge and mindfulness, and he lives detached, and clings to nothing in the world. Thus also, monks, a monk lives contemplating the body in the body.

1.3. Reflection on Repulsiveness of the Body

And further, monks, a monk reflects on this very body enveloped by the skin and full of manifold impurity, from the soles up, and from the top of the head-hairs down, thinking thus: "There are in this body hair of the head, hair of the body, nails, teeth, skin, flesh, sinews, bones, marrow, kidney, heart, liver, midriff, spleen, lungs, intestines, mesentery, gorge, feces, bile, phlegm, pus, blood, sweat, fat, tears, grease, saliva, nasal mucus, synovial fluid, urine."

Just as if there were a double-mouthed provision bag full of various kinds of grain such as hill paddy, paddy, green gram, cow-peas, sesamum, and husked rice, and a man with sound eyes, having opened that bag, were to take stock of the contents thus: "This is hill paddy, this is paddy, this is green gram, this is cow-pea, this is sesamum, this is husked rice." Just so, monks, a monk reflects on this very body enveloped by the skin and full of manifold impurity, from the soles up, and from the top of the head-hairs down, thinking thus: "There are in this body hair of the head, hair of the body, nails, teeth, skin, flesh, sinews, bones, marrow, kidney, heart, liver, midriff, spleen, lungs, intestines, mesentery, gorge, feces, bile, phlegm, pus, blood, sweat, fat, tears, grease, saliva, nasal mucus, synovial fluid, urine."

Thus he lives contemplating the body in the body...

1.4. Reflection on the Material Elements

And further, monks, a monk reflects on this very body, however it be placed or disposed, by way of the material elements: "There are in this body the element of earth, the element of water, the element of fire, the element of wind."

Just as if, monks, a clever cow-butcher or his apprentice, having slaughtered a cow and divided it into portions, should be sitting at the junction of four high roads, in the same way, a monk reflects on this very body, as it is placed or disposed, by way of the material elements: "There are in this body the elements of earth, water, fire, and wind."

Thus he lives contemplating the body in the body...

1.5. The Nine Cemetery Contemplations

1. And further, monks, as if a monk sees a body dead one, two, or three days; swollen, blue and festering, thrown in the charnel ground, he then applies this perception to his own body thus: "Verily, also my own body is of the same nature; such it will become and will not escape it."

   Thus he lives contemplating the body in the body internally, or he lives contemplating the body in the body externally, or he lives contemplating the body in the body internally and externally. He lives contemplating origination-factors in the body, or he lives contemplating dissolution factors in the body, or he lives contemplating origination-and-dissolution-factors in the body. Or his mindfulness is established with the thought: "The body exists," to the extent necessary just for knowledge and mindfulness, and he lives detached, and clings to nothing in the world.

Thus also, monks, a monk lives contemplating the body in the body.

2. And further, monks, as if a monk sees a body thrown in the charnel ground, being eaten by crows, hawks, vultures, dogs, jackals or by different kinds of worms, he then applies this perception to his own body thus: "Verily, also my own body is of the same nature; such it will become and will not escape it."

Thus he lives contemplating the body in the body...

3. And further, monks, as if a monk sees a body thrown in the charnel ground and reduced to a skeleton with some flesh and blood attached to it, held together by the tendons...

4. And further, monks, as if a monk sees a body thrown in the charnel ground and reduced to a skeleton blood-besmeared and without flesh, held together by the tendons...

5. And further, monks, as if a monk sees a body thrown in the charnel ground and reduced to a skeleton without flesh and blood, held together by the tendons...

6. And further, monks, as if a monk sees a body thrown in the charnel ground and reduced to disconnected bones, scattered in all directions here a bone of the hand, there a bone of the foot, a shin bone, a thigh bone, the pelvis, spine, and skull...

7. And further, monks, as if a monk sees a body thrown in the charnel ground, reduced to bleached bones of conch-like color...

8. And further, monks, as if a monk sees a body thrown in the charnel ground reduced to bones, more than a year-old, lying in a heap...

9. And further, monks, as if a monk sees a body thrown in the charnel ground, reduced to bones gone rotten and become dust, he then applies this perception to his own body thus: "Verily, also my own body is of the same nature; such it will become and will not escape it."

Thus he lives contemplating the body in the body internally, or he lives contemplating the body in the body externally, or he lives contemplating the body in the body internally and externally. He lives contemplating origination factors in the body, or he lives contemplating dissolution factors in the body, or he lives contemplating origination-and-dissolution factors in the body. Or his mindfulness is established with the thought: "The body exists," to the extent necessary just for knowledge and mindfulness, and he lives detached, and clings to nothing in the world. Thus also, monks, a monk lives contemplating the body in the body.

ATTAINING THE FOUR JHĀNA STATES

From Samyutta Nikàya 45.8[14] the Buddha describes the levels of meditative absorption (jhana) developed with jhana meditation after sincerely contemplating the body in the body as below,

"Remaining free of distraction by sensuality and

____

14. Can be accessed at the *Becoming Buddha* website: https://becoming-buddha.com/the-jhanas-meditative-absorption/.

sense contact, remaining free of distraction by unskillful mental qualities, entering and remaining in the first jhana: rapture and pleasure born from samadhi, accompanied by directed thought and evaluation (insight).

"With a tranquil mind, (shamatha) entering and remaining in the second jhana: rapture and pleasure born of samadhi, unification of awareness free from directed thought and evaluation, resting in internal assurance. With the fading of rapture, remaining equanimous, mindful and alert, gaining pleasure with the sensation of breathing in the body.

"Entering and remaining in the third jhana, which is equanimous and mindful, a pleasant abiding.

"Abandoning pleasure and pain, due to the renunciation of pleasure and pain, entering and remaining in the fourth jhana: purity of equanimity and mindfulness, neither pleasure nor pain."

* * *

II. CONTEMPLATION OF FEELINGS

And how, monks, does a monk live contemplating feelings in feelings?

Herein, monks, a monk when experiencing a pleasant feeling knows, "I experience a pleasant feeling"; when experiencing a painful feeling, he knows, "I experience a painful feeling"; when experiencing a neither-pleasant-nor-painful feeling," he knows, "I experience a neither-pleasant-nor-painful feeling." When experiencing a pleasant worldly feeling, he knows, "I experience a pleasant worldly feeling"; when experiencing a pleasant spiritual feeling, he knows, "I experience a pleasant spiritual feeling"; when experiencing a painful worldly feeling, he knows, "I experience a painful worldly feeling"; when experiencing a painful spiritual feeling, he knows, "I experience a painful spiritual feeling"; when experiencing a neither-pleasant-nor-painful worldly feeling, he knows, "I experience a neither-pleasant-nor-painful worldly feeling"; when experiencing a neither-pleasant-nor-painful spiritual feeling, he knows, "I experience a neither-pleasant-nor-painful spiritual feeling."

Thus he lives contemplating feelings in feelings internally, or he lives contemplating feelings in feelings externally, or he lives contemplating feelings in feelings internally and externally. He lives contemplating origination factors in feelings, or he lives contemplating dissolution factors in feelings, or he lives contemplating origination-and-dissolution factors in feelings. Or his mindfulness is established with the thought, "Feeling exists," to the extent necessary just for knowledge and mindfulness, and he lives detached, and clings to nothing in the world. Thus, monks, a monk lives contemplating feelings in feelings.

* * *

III. CONTEMPLATION OF CONSCIOUSNESS

And how, monks, does a monk live contemplating consciousness in consciousness?

Herein, monks, a monk knows the consciousness with lust, as with lust; the consciousness without lust, as without lust; the consciousness with hate, as with hate; the consciousness without hate, as without hate; the consciousness with ignorance, as with ignorance; the consciousness without ignorance, as without ignorance; the shrunken state of consciousness, as the shrunken state; the distracted state of consciousness, as the distracted state; the developed state of consciousness as the developed state; the undeveloped state of consciousness as the undeveloped state; the state of consciousness with some other mental state superior to it, as the state with something mentally higher; the state of consciousness with no other mental state superior to it, as the state with nothing mentally higher; the concentrated state of consciousness, as the concentrated state; the unconcentrated state of consciousness, as the unconcentrated state; the freed state of consciousness, as the freed state; and the unfreed state of consciousness as the unfreed state.

Thus he lives contemplating consciousness in consciousness internally, or he lives contemplating consciousness in consciousness externally, or he lives contemplating consciousness in consciousness internally and externally. He lives contemplating origination factors in consciousness, or he lives contemplating dissolution-factors in consciousness, or he lives contemplating origination-and-dissolution factors in consciousness. Or his mindfulness is established with the thought, "Consciousness exists," to the extent necessary just for knowledge and mindfulness, and he lives detached, and clings to nothing in the world. Thus, monks, a monk lives contemplating consciousness in consciousness.

* * *

IV. CONTEMPLATION OF MENTAL OBJECTS

4.1. The Five Hindrances

And how, monks, does a monk live contemplating mental objects in mental objects?

Herein, monks, a monk lives contemplating mental objects in the mental objects of the five hindrances.

Herein, monks, when *sense-desire* is present, a monk knows, "There is sense-desire in me," or when sense-desire is not present, he knows, "There is no sense-desire in me." He knows how the arising of the non-arisen sense-desire comes to be; he knows how the abandoning of the arisen sense-desire comes to be; and he knows how the non-arising in the future of the abandoned sense-desire comes to be.

When *anger* is present, he knows, "There is anger in me," or when anger is not present, he knows, "There is no anger in me." He knows how the arising of the non-arisen anger comes to be; he knows how the abandoning of the arisen anger comes to be; and he knows how the non-arising in the future of the abandoned anger comes to be.

When *sloth and torpor* are present, he knows, "There are sloth and torpor in me," or when sloth and torpor are not present, he knows, "There are no sloth and torpor in me." He knows how the arising of the non-arisen sloth and torpor comes to be; he knows how the abandoning of the arisen sloth and torpor comes to be; and he knows how the non-arising in the future of the abandoned sloth and torpor comes to be.

When *agitation and remorse* are present, he knows, "There are agitation and remorse in me," or when agitation and remorse are not present, he knows, "There are no agitation and remorse in me." He knows how the arising of the non-arisen agitation and remorse comes to be; he knows how the abandoning of the arisen agitation and remorse comes to be; and he knows how the non-arising in the future of the abandoned agitation and remorse comes to be.

When *doubt* is present, he knows, "There is doubt in me," or when doubt is not present, he knows, "There is no doubt in me." He knows how the arising of the non-arisen doubt comes to be; he knows how the abandoning of the arisen doubt comes to be; and he knows how the non-arising in the future of the abandoned doubt comes to be.

4. 2. The Five Aggregates of Clinging

1. And further, monks, a monk lives contemplating mental objects in the mental objects of the five

aggregates of clinging.

2. How, monks, does a monk live contemplating mental objects in the mental objects of the five aggregates of clinging?

3. Herein, monks, a monk thinks, "Thus is material form; thus is the arising of material form; and thus is the disappearance of material form. Thus is feeling; thus is the arising of feeling; and thus is the disappearance of feeling. Thus is perception; thus is the arising of perception; and thus is the disappearance of perception. Thus are formations; thus is the arising of formations; and thus is the disappearance of formations. Thus is consciousness; thus is the arising of consciousness; and thus is the disappearance of consciousness."

4.3. Six Internal and External Bases

How, monks, does a monk live contemplating mental objects in the mental objects of the six internal and the six external sense-bases?

Herein, monks, a monk knows the eye and visual forms and the fetter that arises dependent on both (the eye and forms); he knows how the arising of the non-arisen fetter comes to be; he knows how the abandoning of the arisen fetter comes to be; and he knows how the non-arising in the future of the abandoned fetter comes to be.

He knows the *ear* and *sounds*... the *nose* and *smells*... the *tongue* and *flavors*... the *body* and *tactual objects*... the *mind* and *mental objects,* and the fetter that arises dependent on both; he knows how the arising of the non-arisen fetter comes to be; he knows how the abandoning of the arisen fetter comes to be; and he knows how the non-arising in the future of the abandoned fetter comes to be.

4.4. The Seven Factors of Enlightenment

And further, monks, a monk lives contemplating mental objects in the mental objects of the seven factors of enlightenment.

How, monks, does a monk live contemplating mental objects in the mental objects of the seven factors of enlightenment?

1. Herein, monks, when the enlightenment-factor of mindfulness is present, the monk knows, "The enlightenment-factor of mindfulness is in me," or when the enlightenment-factor of mindfulness is absent, he knows, "The enlightenment-factor of mindfulness is not in me"; and he knows how the arising of the non-arisen enlightenment-factor of mindfulness comes to be; and how perfection in the development of the arisen enlightenment-factor of mindfulness comes to be.

2. When the enlightenment-factor of the investigation of mental objects is present, the monk knows, "The enlightenment-factor of the investigation of mental objects is in me"; when the enlightenment-factor of the investigation of mental objects is absent, he knows, "The enlightenment-factor of the investigation of mental objects is not in me"; and he knows how the arising of the non-arisen

enlightenment-factor of the investigation of mental objects comes to be, and how perfection in the development of the arisen enlightenment-factor of the investigation of mental objects comes to be.

3. When the enlightenment-factor of energy is present, he knows, "The enlightenment-factor of energy is in me"; when the enlightenment-factor of energy is absent, he knows, "The enlightenment-factor of energy is not in me"; and he knows how the arising of the non-arisen enlightenment-factor of energy comes to be, and how perfection in the development of the arisen enlightenment-factor of energy comes to be.

4. When the enlightenment-factor of joy is present, he knows, "The enlightenment-factor of joy is in me"; when the enlightenment-factor of joy is absent, he knows, "The enlightenment-factor of joy is not in me"; and he knows how the arising of the non-arisen enlightenment-factor of joy comes to be, and how perfection in the development of the arisen enlightenment-factor of joy comes to be.

5. When the enlightenment-factor of tranquility is present, he knows, "The enlightenment-factor of tranquility is in me"; when the enlightenment-factor of tranquility is absent, he knows, "The enlightenment-factor of tranquility is not in me"; and he knows how the arising of the non-arisen enlightenment-factor of tranquility comes to be, and how perfection in the development of the arisen enlightenment-factor of tranquility comes to be.

6. When the enlightenment-factor of concentration is present, he knows, "The enlightenment-factor of concentration is in me"; when the enlightenment-factor of concentration is absent, he knows, "The enlightenment-factor of concentration is not in me"; and he knows how the arising of the non-arisen enlightenment-factor of concentration comes to be, and how perfection in the development of the arisen enlightenment-factor of concentration comes to be.

7. When the enlightenment-factor of equanimity is present, he knows, "The enlightenment-factor of equanimity is in me"; when the enlightenment-factor of equanimity is absent, he knows, "The enlightenment-factor of equanimity is not in me"; and he knows how the arising of the non-arisen enlightenment-factor of equanimity comes to be, and how perfection in the development of the arisen enlightenment-factor of equanimity comes to be.

4.5. The Four Noble Truths

And further, monks, a monk lives contemplating mental objects in the mental objects of the four noble truths.

How, monks, does a monk live contemplating mental objects in the mental objects of the four noble truths?

Herein, monks, a monk knows, *"This is suffering,"* according to reality; he knows, *"This is the origin of suffering,"* according to reality; he knows, *"This is the cessation of suffering,"* according to reality; he knows *"This is the road leading to the cessation of suffering,"* according to reality.

1. Suffering

   Birth, old age, illness, death, separation of love, meeting of hatred and enmity, failure to achieve what one wishes for, suffering of the flourishing of the Five Skandhas.

2. The origin of suffering

   Craving leads to rebirth. Go with joy and greed, seek here and there-for example, desire for desire, desire for existence, and non-existence.

   Monks! Where does craving arise? Where to stay?

   - Whatever form is dear, whatever form is lovable, craving arises there, abides there.

   - Eyes, ears, nose, tongue, body, mind; Sight, sound, smell, taste, touch, dharma. If it is lovable, craving arises there and abides there.

   - Eye consciousness, ear consciousness, nose consciousness, tongue consciousness, body consciousness, consciousness; Eye contact, ear contact, eye contact, tongue contact, body contact, mind contact; Feeling of the eye, the feeling of the ear, feeling of the nose, feeling of the tongue, feeling of the body, feeling of the mind. If it is lovable,. Craving arises there and abides there.

   - Perception of form, perception of sound, perception of smell, perception of taste, perception of touch, perception of dharma;

Thoughts of form, sound, scent, taste, touch, dharma; Love for form, love for sound, love for scent, love for taste, love for touch, love for dharma; Thought of form, thought of sound, thought of scent, thought of taste, thought of touch, thought of dharma; Four of form, four of sound, four of scent, four of taste, four of touch, four of dharma. If it is lovable, craving arises there and abides there.

3. The cessation of suffering

- Eliminate craving, have no regrets, and be completely liberated. Where to let go of craving? Where to eradicate?

- In life, whatever forms are dear, whatever forms are lovable, craving for renunciation is there. There is an end to it.

4. The path of cessation of suffering: This is the Eightfold Path.

(1) Right view: Seeing and knowing about suffering, origin, cessation, and path.

(2) Right thinking: Thinking about leaving desire, anger, avoiding harmful thoughts.

(3) Right speech: Do not lie, avoid double-tongued, negative words, and embellishment.

(4) Right action: Do not kill, steal, or commit adultery.

(5) Right livelihood: Not supporting oneself by means of cultivating the three poisons of greed,

anger, and ignorance.

(6) Right effort: Effort, not allowing negative dharmas to arise. If negativity has arisen, let it dissipate. The positive consequences that have not yet arisen, let them arise. The positive is born and we let it grow.

(7) Right mindfulness: Be diligent and aware of the Four Foundations of Mindfulness.

(8) Right concentration:

- First jhāna: Joy and ease arise from directed thought and evaluation (insight).

- Second jhāna: Extermination of thoughts, joy and ease arise from concentration, directed thought and evaluation, resting in internal assurance.

- Third jhāna: Detachment, equanimous and mindful, a pleasant abiding.

- Fourth jhāna: Abandoning pleasure and pain, due to the renunciation of pleasure and pain. The purity of equanimity and mindfulness, neither pleasure nor pain.

Thus he lives contemplating mental objects in mental objects internally, or he lives contemplating mental objects in mental objects externally, or he lives contemplating mental objects in mental objects internally and externally. He lives contemplating origination-factors in mental objects, or he lives contemplating dissolution-factors in mental objects, or he lives contemplating origination-and-dissolution-factors in mental objects. Or his mindfulness is established with the thought,

"Mental objects exist," to the extent necessary just for knowledge and mindfulness, and he lives detached, and clings to nothing in the world. Thus, monks, a monk lives contemplating mental objects in the mental objects of the four noble truths.

Verily, monks, whosoever practices these four foundations of mindfulness in this manner for maximum of seven years or one to six years or even only six months, then one of these two fruits may be expected by him: highest knowledge (arahantship) here and now, or if some remainder of clinging is yet present, the state of non-returning.

Because of this it was said: "This is the only way, monks, for the purification of beings, for the overcoming of sorrow and lamentation, for the destruction of suffering and grief, for reaching the right path, for the attainment of Nibbana, namely the four foundations of mindfulness."

Thus spoke the Blessed One. Satisfied, the monks approved of his words.

* * *

GENERAL IDEAS

Definition the Four Foundations of Mindfulness: mindfulness of the body, of feelings, of the mind, and of dharmas. We can constantly reflect and investigate these four foundations.

Sanskrit	Pali	Vietnamese
Smrti	Sati	Niệm
Upasthana	Upatthana	Xứ
Smrtyupasthana	Satipaṭṭhāna	Niệm Xứ

The Four Foundations of Mindfulness are the gateway to enlightenment and hold a central position in Buddhism. Generation after generation, the Four Foundations of Mindfulness are learned, practiced, and propagated with great care.

I. CONTEMPLATION OF THE BODY

Practitioner contemplates:

Breath

Body posture

Body movements

Parts of the body

Elements are composed the body

Destruction of the body.

II. THE CONTEMPLATION OF FEELING

1. Three feelings: suffering, pleasure, neutral.

   The feeling of suffering: The mental suffering and physical suffering (double miseries).

   The feeling of pleasure: Suffering caused by impermanence.

The feeling of neutrality: Neither suffering nor pleasure.

2. The feeling of birth, existence, change and disappearance (impermanence).

III. THE CONTEMPLATION OF CONSCIOUSNESS

The practitioners observe that greed, anger, and ignorance arise and disappear, generous or narrow-minded, calm or chaotic, binding or liberating. Each state of mind is self-aware.

IV. CONTEMPLATION OF MENTAL OBJECTS

- Five hindrances: Desire, anger, restlessness, torpor, indecisiveness (undecided).

- Five aggregates of clinging: Form, feeling, perception, mental formations, consciousness.

- Eighteen objects (dhātu): Six sense organs, six worldly objects and six consciousnesses.

- Seven Factors of Enlightenment: Mindfulness, the investigation of mental objects, energy, joy, tranquility, concentration, and equanimity.

- Four Noble Truths: suffering, origin, cessation, path.

Happiness and liberation are two elements: if this is, that is, and if this is not, that is not. Practicing meditation can achieve peace and liberation right in the moment of practice. The nature of greed, anger, worry, and fear is all ignorance.

First, we need to be aware of them and then contemplate and examine both. Gradually ignorance disappears, and the observing mind (vipassana) and the illuminated scene become one, because we are not the observer, but we are observing ourselves.

* * *

THE ORIGIN

In ancient times, the Buddhist scriptures in Northern India were compiled in Sanskrit.

Southern Indian scriptures are compiled in Pali script. Both Sanskrit and Pali versions of the Four Foundations of Mindfulness Sutta spread to Vietnam.

The suttas we are studying belong to the Sarvastivada sect, translated from Sanskrit into Chinese at the end of the fourth century. In1960, Zen Master Thanh Từ translated it into Vietnamese.

In the Sanskrit Canon, the Satipaṭṭhāna Sutta is number 98 in the Majjhima Agama and number 26 in the Taisho Tripitaka. The Ekottarāgama number 12 also has this sutta but titles it Nhất Nhập Đạo Phẩm in Vietnamese. Zen Master Thích Nhat Hanh translated it into Vietnamese, called Con Đường Vào Đạo Duy Nhất in Vietnamese.

The Satipaṭṭhāna Sutta is number 10 of the Majjhima

Nikaya and number 22 of the Digha Nikaya in the Pali Canon.

The Pali Pitaka belongs to the Theravada sect, a sect that has maintained the complete Tripitaka, thanks to its relatively safe practice area in Sri Lanka. The Pali sutta entitled The Foundations of Mindfulness was translated by Venerable Minh Chau in 1970.

***

PREPARING TO PRACTICE

(Excerpt from Đường Về Niết Bàn, The Road to Nirvana)

1. Find a qualified Zen master.

2. Practice the Four Right Efforts. Always observe the mistakes of the five desires (form, sound, smell, taste, touch) and the five emotions (greed, anger, torpor, restlessness, and doubt).

3. Stop worrying. Try to do less of three things: eating, talking, and sleeping. Avoid being busy. Find a quiet place to stay. Have enough neccessary things to practice.

4. Strictly maintain the precepts and protect the six senses.

5. Keep the middle way: Do not be too lenient or too strict. Sit cross-legged, half-lotus, or on a chair as long as it is comfortable. But remember: if it is too

comfortable, it can easily make you sleepy.

6. Faith and reason, diligence, and calmness. These two pairs must be balanced like a charioteer keeping two horses running parallel.

7. During the session, the inner mind must be constantly absorbed, but outside of the session, try to always be insightful, light and maintain a dignified posture.

* * *

THE PROCEDURE AT EVERY COURSE

1. Praise the Three Jewels. Make a solemn ceremony to invite the Zen master to guide.

2. May parents, teachers, and all sentient beings be free from all suffering and be happy forever.

3. The contemplation of impermanence: We are lucky to be born as human beings and meeting the Buddha Dharma. These are all good causes and conditions that are difficult to encounter but easy to pass.

4. The Four Foundations of Mindfulness is the common path of all sages. May we follow it until the day we attain enlightenment.

* * *

THE ADVICE

(By Zen Master Mahasi in the book, The Practice of Vipassana Meditation)

If you feel pain or discomfort and have noted it, the pain keeps increasing. Please do neither, no panic nor fear.

Return the attention to your breathing. You have a feeling of difficulty breathing. Sometimes, it feels like being pricked by a needle or tickled like worms are crawling inside you; sometimes it hurts like something bitten, sometimes shaking as with malaria. If you stop meditating, it will go away, and when you meditate, it will appear again. It is not morbid or spooky. Normally, you are so busy that you do not pay attention. Now our mind is calm and clear, you can feel it. If you stop meditating, when you start practicing again, you will continue to have to confront these feelings. If you persevere in meditation, you will overcome it. Many times, you see your body shaking or trembling, do not be afraid or excited, just pay attention and note it until it stops. If it does not go away, you should lie down and rest but continue to meditate. Only with patience, will there will be success. Meditation progresses, sometimes with tremors or chills in the spine or whole body. It is a state of bliss that signals a good outcome.

According to the ancient tradition, Zen masters often advise practitioners to put their trust in the Buddha and not to panic whenever unhealthy or scary images appear. Just sit for fifteen or thirty minutes to practice.

Gradually takes longer depending on ability. You should create a habit of meditating every day.

* * *

THE EXERCISE

I. CONTEMPLATION OF THE BODY

Breathe consciously. Breathe in, know how to breathe in; breathe out, know how to breathe out. Every ten breaths without confusion is a significant step. The effect comes back to us. The illusory thoughts arise and we can see we have been distracted. Continuous practice determines success.

Breathe in long and know how to breathe in long. Breathe out long, know how to breathe out long.

Breathe in short, know how to breathe in short. Breathe out short, know how to breathe out short.

The mind is identical to the entire length of the breath; do not let a stray thought interfere. It is called depending on the breath method. Breathing is regular, smooth, and gentle, then body and mind are relaxed and happy.

Feel the body breathing in. Feel the body exhale.

Every day we live in one body, but our mind runs another way. Now our body and mind are unified. If the body sits firmly, the muscles are relaxed, and the breathing is moderate, the nerves will be calm, and the mind will be at peace.

Calming down our whole body, we breathe in.

Calming down my whole body, I breathe out.

Use your breathing to regulate your heart rate; thereby calming your nerves and helping whole body function safely. Breathing smoothly, without noise, is a sign of good health. The more subtle the breath, the more peaceful the body and mind. Breathing in your body relaxes. Breathing out and all the tiredness and sadness disappear. Close all six sense doors, return to the breath, return to yourselves. Feelings of happiness have a nourishing effect.

Bhikkhus walk, stand, lie down, and sit, knowing clearly how their body is used. The bhikkhu walks back and forth, puts on his robe, carries the bowl, washes the bowl, and is aware of every movement of his body. For example: When walking, he must pay attention to the movement of his legs. The mind should observe "lift." Then, a foot lifted off the ground. The mind notes "step." The feet raise up and then down. The mind notes "putting." Then the feet "put down." Both the right and left are the same. After walking a distance, at the end of the road, the mind notes wanting to turn, and then the body turns in a different direction.

During meals, the mind notes "scoop." Then hands "take" the soup. The mind orders "pass to mouth."Then the hand brings food to the mouth. The mind observes "pass to mouth" when bringing food to the lips. The mind notes that the food enters the mouth. The mind says "shut," and the mouth is closed. Chewing, swallowing, putting hands down . . . observe each movement.

The body can only move according to clear understanding of the mind, not indiscriminately according to habit. Force your mind to practice being alert in the present moment, not distracting yourself with thoughts of the past and future. The mind records every movement, more or less, depending on each person's level of insight, and depending on the situation, to be leisurely or hasty. The only important thing is whether we pay attention or not. The above exercises train the mind to calm down on the breath and not chase the six sense objects. This method is called samatha (stopping). Now, we practice observing our body and mind. This method is called vipassana (contemplation). The meditation of no-thought can lead to the formless heaven. However, wisdom cannot arise. So, we do not say that concentration gives wisdom, but we must say that the right concentration can give rise to wisdom. The right meditation is the concentration that uses both samatha and vipassana methods.

Vipassana meditation not only uses breathing to stabilize but also uses wisdom to see the impermanence and non-self of the body and mind. Therefore, this eliminates the three poisons of greed, anger, and ignorance, which are a heavy yoke that we have been wearing for many lifetimes. The current fruit of vipassana is that the practitioner becomes calm, dignified and mindful in all movements and language.

THIRTY-TWO BODY PARTS

- Hair, body hair, nails, teeth, skin.

- Meat, tendons, bones, marrow, kidneys.

- Heart, liver, mucous membrane, stomach, spleen, lungs.

- Large intestine, small intestine, feces, brain, bile.

- Phlegm, pus, blood, sweat, thick fat, liquid fat.

- Tears, snot, saliva, mucus, urine.

First, learn by heart each phrase forward and backward. Then, memorize all thirty-two forward and backwards. Keep reading until you enter one state of concentration. If you cannot calm down, you must observe each part in its aspects: form, color, position, illness, and dirt, to know how to get bored with false phenomenun. Contemplate the thirty-two body parts as well as the following two exercises that are not coordinated with the breath.

Observe in the body the solid things that belong to the earth, the flowing things that belong to the water, the hot things that belong to fire, the movements that belong to the wind, the emptiness that belongs to space, the distinctions that belong to the consciousness. Observe the interrelationship between us and all things. The sun is outside this body, but without the sun, this body could not live. Our life is not only present in the body. The habit view that this body is Me, is Mine, I am only in this body, is a wrong view.

Observe the impermanent and certain destruction of

the body:

1. The corpse is crushed.

2. Dogs and vultures rustle.

3. The skeleton is covered with flesh.

4. Out of meat, only blood remains.

5. Out of meat and out of blood.

6. Bone falls off.

7. Bones change color.

8. Rotten bones.

9. Dust.

Having the courage to look at the truth of the body will help you stop being pessimistic and know how to appreciate life. How to avoid wasting your human life and realize how hard it is to have it. This method of contemplation on impurity eliminates self-cherishing and with it, all diseases of greed, anger, and ignorance are ended. Cultivators, because of the Right View, are liberated, and because of peace, they are happy.

Review the above eight lessons with the intention of realizing the nature of birth and death (impermanence) and dependent origination (non-self) of all dharmas. This awakening liberates all greed and anxiety. People suffer not because the world is impermanent and non-self but only because they obscure that truth, causing troubles to arise. Just like the five aggregates are inherently errorless, the root of falling is in attachment (the five aggregates of clinging) as true (I and mine).

People practicing the Four Foundations of Mindfulness are not attached to anything, so they are relaxed and happy, neither struggling to chase after things nor running away. Because these practitioners always use vipassana to face old age, sickness, and death, they become familiar with the changes of old age, sickness, and death, so they are not afraid. Contemplating all things is not to reject all things but to contact all things with wisdom.

The Four Foundations of Mindfulness do not struggle with greed, anger, and ignorance. The Four Foundations of Mindfulness opens the wisdom—like lighting a lamp so that darkness turns into light without having to bother chasing the darkness away.

* * *

II. CONTEMPLATION OF FEELINGS

(Breathing in) knows that the painful feelings have arisen. (Breathing out) knows that painful feelings are present. (Breathing in) knows that the pleasant feelings have arisen. (Breathing out) knows the feelings of pleasure are staying.

Practice identifying feelings: suffering (painful feeling), happiness (pleasure feeling), neither suffering nor joy (neutral feeling). Whenever there is a suffering feeling, neither chase it away, nor stay away, calmly follow your breathing, and note the rising of suffering, the increase of suffering, the lessening of suffering, or the cessation of suffering.

Whenever there is a happy or ignorant feeling, practice contemplation, do not get attached, do not get involved, and do not take it for granted that you are happy, but clearly see that this is a feeling that arises due to conditions (the cause is self-love, the condition is the external scene).

Neither being attached nor abandoning is called equanimity. Equanimity is one of the four immeasurable minds (love, compassion, sympathetic joy, and equanimity).

The river is moving water drops. Our body is a river. Boundless cells are transforming. Our mind is also a river. Feelings arise and disappear continuously, according to the activities of the six senses. The pleasure feeling leads to attachment. The misery feeling leads to boredom. Every feeling stimulates greed or anger to arise. Now, with mindfulness, the situation begins to change. Feelings evolve under the light of consciousness.

Mindfulness does not recognize it as us anymore, does not say "I like this, I dislike that, I'm happy, or I'm miserable." The first effect is to restore our sovereignty, so the feeling has lost 80 percent of its magic power.

The second effect is to see its origin as ignorance. Because of clinging to the ego and mine, there is feeling. The third effect is to know that its nature is illusory, without essence, just feelings that arise and disappear according to causes and conditions. For example, being grumpy and frowning all day is due to staying up late and lacking sleep. It is the misery feeling originating from physiology. Sometimes, we get angry because we misunderstand a friend. It is rooted in psychology. Sometimes when we see a mess in the house, we get angry. It is the suffering feeling from the physical. Being praised makes us happy, so we contemplate or reflect, and discover that the basis of happiness is self-cherishing. This feeling of pleasure leads to illusion. Only by awakening can we avoid useless pride and complacency. The illusion of happiness disappears and gives way to healthy joy that nourishes enlightenment.

Feelings are clear and uncertain. Suffering and happiness depend on each person's nature. For Mr. A, working is torture. But for Mr. B, sitting idle is very uncomfortable. Having a stuffy nose and then being able to breathe is nothing more than happiness. Tens of thousands of such factors of happiness go unnoticed. We keep accidentally trampling on happiness to find happiness. When it passes, you will suffer from regret.

The Buddha taught us to use our breath to reflect on the presence of suffering and joy and then gradually overcome it. You are breathing gently, calmly, and gradually. The body and mind gradually become calm and peaceful. Just like that, we purify all three feelings. The right view clearly sees the origin, nature, and consequences of painful and happy feelings, thus liberating them from their control.

* * *

III. CONTEMPLATION OF CONSCIOUSNESS

There are many mental factors, but the scriptures only mention twenty-two. The method of contemplating the mind is the same as contemplating feelings. One you know the origin, nature, and consequences of mental states, you will immediately be liberated.

1. Contemplation on desire:

    Craving for sight, sound, smell, taste, and touch is called the five desires. Greed for money, beauty, prestige, good food, and lots of sleep are called the five vulgar desires. The disease of greed is difficult to cure because it is sweet and attractive. The Buddha taught that the desire is a pit of burning coals, which sick people mistake for warmth and happiness. The sutta teaches as below:

    When there is no presence of desire, the practitioner also notes clearly.

    (Breathe in) now the mind is not greedy. (Exhale) now the mind is not greedy.

    Find the source of this absence. Remember the ease that comes with this absence.

2. Contemplation on anger:

    The first benefit is the experience of having anger and losing peace. Excessive anger leading to hatred is the factor leading to hell in present and future. The danger of anger is that it stimulates the body, mouth, and mind to go down a negative path. Once the anger is identified, this negative mental factor immediately reduces its harmful nature.

(Breathing in) know that anger has arisen. (Breathing out) know that anger is present. (Breathing in) know that anger has subsided. (Breathing out) know that anger has disappeared.

The mindfulness restores autonomy. Anger calms down and a cool, refreshing feeling appears called non-anger. The anger is converted into compassion. Among the five skandhas, the anger causing irritation and discomfort is the skandha of feelings (the cover of senses), the arising of thoughts is the skandha of perception, the transformation of the mind is the skandha of actions, the nature present in mental seeds are the skandhas of consciousness, their figures that appear are the skandhas of forms.

* * *

Meditation gives us ability to transform the defilements into bodhi. Most people are often tired of dirty trash and love roses.

Gardeners know that from compost to roses and from roses to compost, they use both. The Buddha made a vow: "Infinite sentient beings will be saved because in his dharma eye, he clearly sees the incomparable saint and mortal.

Mindfulness is like a lamp that illuminates the near and far causes of anger (misunderstandings, pride, doubt, irritable nerves, lack of sympathy, educational circumstances, customs, and psychology). These roots are present in both ourselves and others, increasing the negative conditions for ignorance.

Seeing and understanding is the foundation for freeing anger, bringing the nectar of compassion to build and heal what anger has broken.

There are wise people who, every time they are angry, go to their room and sit quietly to avoid the harmful consequences of an insecure body and mouth. Of course, the anger will gradually subside. But if it is not exposed, the roots will sink deeper into the subconscious, waiting for the right conditions to burst out again.

People who practice the Four Foundations of Mindfulness use their breath to return to mindfulness, not worrying about the other person. As soon as negative actions and cruel words appear, they disappear. We let it dissolve according to its impermanent nature. Because we often kept thinking about it, it will burn down our mental house.

To calm our mind, we breathe in. We breathe out to calm our mind.

We woke up and realized that the person who harmed us was an illusory anger. Cool again, we can pass this coolness to the other person and reconcile together. In the past, the Buddha and ancestors had their hands and feet cut off without anger because the patience and wisdom go hand in hand. Now we know that sounds and appearances are all false. our body and other people's bodies are just soil, water, wind, and fire, so there is no humiliation to endure.

3. The Contemplation of compassion:

To treat anger, we must practice the method of compassion. Loving means giving peace and forgiving the mistakes of others. Compassion is to save others from suffering. Metta's nature is tolerance, wishing the best for everyone. The nature of compassion is the wisdom of understanding the suffering of others and developing the intention to save them.

Observing the eight sufferings,15 observing physical and mental suffering, will open the source of compassion.

Contemplation of compassion does not only have the effect of benefiting others. Bring peace and joy to others and eliminate disasters yourself. Any action or word that comes from a compassionate mind, wanting to relieve the suffering of people or things, will bring present and future happiness to yourself. The sutta says: A spoonful of rice soup with your compassion for the sick has more merit than water in the Atlantic Ocean.

We can spread compassion in the four directions to all living beings. The aura of compassion has the ability to travel as far as sound and light.

With the substance of compassion in the heart, a

---

15. Eight Sufferings: (1) Suffering of Birth (2) Suffering of old age (3) Suffering of sickness (4) Suffering of death (5) Suffering of being apart from the loved ones (6) Suffering being together with the despised ones (7) Suffering of not getting what one wants (8) Suffering of the flourishing of the five skandhas.

word, a facial expression, or a look, will have the miracle of making withered hearts restore faith and live happily.

* * *

IV. CONTEMPLATION OF MENTAL OBJECTS

1. Five hindrances: five heavy mental factors that cover the mind like a black curtain covering a lamp.

   The five are craving, anger, torpor, restlessness, and doubt about the Dharma. The bhikkhu examines the mind, when one of the five arises, he immediately finds a method to eliminate it to prevent rebirth.

   The Five Skandhas: The bhikkhu examines and identifies: This is form, this is feeling, this is perception, this is action, this is consciousness. Let the five uses of the mind arise and then disappear naturally on their own, like guests coming and going. Practice separating from us and the five, looking at them appearing then disappearing, without us inside.

2. Contemplate the eighteen objects (dhatu): Six sense organs face six **worldly objects** that give birth to six consciousnesses. The practitioner knows the internal formations that arise, abide, change, and die. Neither get excited, nor get fooled. Separate each sense, object, and consciousness to clearly see the meaning of dependent-origination. Whether spiritual or material, there is no thing that is not based on other dharmas and depends on other dharmas, so every

dharma has no self-nature (selflessness).

- Hindrance: It has the same meaning as habit and karma. The knot is tied. Order is to command as the habit.

- The five slow hindrances: Five serious karma that is slow but deep and difficult to get rid of: Greed, anger, ignorance, arrogance, and doubt. They order us to do wrong.

- The five fast hindrances: The five hindrances command us very quick but easy to wake up. They are self-view, part view, wrong view, prejudice, and clinging to precepts.

Because six sense organs and six **worldly objects** are not faulty, one should contemplate the mental objects in the mental objects here and be aware of the arising, existence, and transformation of the internal hindrances. The collective life of monks and nuns is very convenient for awakening the hidden hindrance potentials in the mind. Only by seeing the hindrance enemy and knowing where it is can we transform it. These arbitrary bonds have been steeped in the bottom of our mind and they still secrete poison into our daily language and thoughts. Only through meditation and mindful contemplation can we see their traces. Therefore, the Brief Four Parts of the Vinaya (Tứ Phần Luật Lược Ghi) has the sentences:

Even if the nature of precepts is not violated, it can only control the harshness of the body and mouth, but the mind still has the subtle and easy inclination to violate the precepts. As for subtle afflictions, we are still in the desire realm. Whenever we have strictly kept the pure precepts, knowing how to establish your will in meditation, gain the four jhana states, the four great pure realms of form that manifest themselves in the body, then it is called goodness.

Treating guilt and fear: Regret is uncertain. Sometimes it is beneficial, and sometimes it is an obstacle. Recognize your mistakes, determined to let them go. It is over, let's go on a good path from now on. If your guilt continues to haunt you, how can you practice peacefully? It is an obstacle.

Fear is also an important internal hindrance; the substance is ignorance. Those who have experience in spiritual practice, all affirm that fear goes hand in hand with self-grasping. Contemplation of the impurity body is a 100 percent effective medicine for fearlessness.

(1) Seven Factors of Enlightenment: Mindfulness, the investigation of mental objects, energy, joy, tranquility, concentration, and equanimity. A bhikkhu contemplates in his mind, that if he does not have these seven supporting factors, he must practice for them to arise. If he has it, he will maintain it and know how to use it.

(2) The Four Noble Truths: Suffering, origin, cessation, and path. Cultivate these four pearls of wisdom until the decisive achievement.

* * *

FINAL ADVICE

In the Majjhima Agama, the Buddha taught Rahula to meditate on seven topics when he was eighteen years old:

- Allow the positive to arise to eliminate negative intentions.

- Recite compassion to eliminate cruelty.

- Reflect on joy to eliminate anger.

- Remember eequanimity to eliminate hatred.

- Meditate on impurity to eliminate the three poisons of greed, anger, and ignorance.

- Contemplate impermanence to release pride and self-love.

- Focus on breathing to regulate both body and mind.

The Buddha taught: "The awakened person, night, and day, carefully and completely directs his mind to the Dharma. Hey monks! Regardless of the situation or what you are doing, mindfulness is still essential."

Although listening to lectures and studying suttas is the right thing to do, the important thing is still in practice. Self-contemplation, self-reflection, and self-invention, be diligent and do not close your eyes and get lost in leisure. Without practice, wisdom cannot shine. Without true seeing and understanding, there is no liberation. Venerable Huong Nghiem asked Patriarch Quy Son a question. The Patriarch replied: "If I reply to it, you will blame me later." Huong Nghiem was very upset and left the temple to go somewhere else. Thirty years of pondering that one sentence of the Patriarch. One day, while hoeing the ground, a pebble was thrown into the bamboo tree, making a "click" sound. He suddenly had great enlightenment, quickly took a bath, dressed neatly, lit three incense sticks towards Quy Son mountain, bowed, and made offerings, thanking him for not saying anything. This means the enlightenment came from inside, not simply from words.

Since ancient times, the patriarchs have successfully attained enlightenment because of their perseverance and self-reliance in meditating every moment without rest, year after year without fatigue or discouragement. The Four Foundations of Mindfulness Sutta includes many methods. Beginners should obey the Buddha and learn everything. The contemplations is to unlock wisdom. Regulate your breathing to calm down. There are three types of irregular breathing:

a. Wind: Breathing in and out makes a sound.

b. Asthma: Stagnation, breathing is not clear.

c. Air: Not gentle. The gentle breath is called the breath that makes it easy to calm down. The wind is moving. Asthma is stagnant. Air is laborious. Focusing on these three types is not only useless but also harmful.

How to cure:

(1) Let go of all predestined thoughts, be single minded.

(2) Relax your body, move in and out naturally

without restraint.

(3) Imagine the whole body breathing together, the breath going in and out through the pores smoothly. Enough of these three things, from the gross to the subtle, naturally the mind is concentrated, and the body is at peace.

Concentration and wisdom are the two wheels of a vehicle, the two wings of a bird. Meditation without wisdom is a delusion. Only studying wisdom without meditation lead to madness. The harm of a one-wheeled vehicle and a one-winged bird is truly pitiful. It is easy to talk in depth, but if you want to really understand the subtleties, you have to put in a lot of effort in practicing meditation. When the practice is effective, the practitioner who wants to enter concentration can freely choose a subject and diligently enter it. The means is the way to the destination. The ancients taught: "A ten thousand feet high tower must come from the ground." This statement is very sincere.

Mind is a common noun for the human spirit. Consciousness is the distinguishing function of the mind. Intention is the karma-creating function of the mind. Because intention stimulates words and deeds. If the intention is greed, anger, and ignorance, the karma will be painful. If you want to be happy, the main role of the mind must be to live a pure life as taught in verse one and two of the Dhammapada:

"Mind precedes all mental states. Mind is their chief; they are all mind-wrought. If with an impure mind a person speaks or acts suffering follows him like the wheel that follows the foot of the ox.

Mind precedes all mental states. Mind is their chief; they are all mind-wrought. If with a pure mind a person speaks or acts happiness follows him like his never-departing shadow."

(Dhammapada, Verse 1–2)[16]

The Buddha advises us to look inward, mainly to regularly purify our minds. Therefore, our words, actions, and actions become naturally pure and good.

So, looking inward is to look outward in a good, purely moral way which leads us and other people to be forever happy in the present and future.

* * *

THE UNDEFILED LEAF BRANCHES

The vast sea is covered with white waves. The wind is the cause that makes the water rise. The stronger the wind, the bigger the waves, chasing each other noisily into creation and destruction. Our true mind is like the ocean. The delusional thoughts arise like thousands of waves rushing continuously. We forget the vastness of our minds and accept false thoughts as our minds.

Venerable Anan listened to the Buddha declare: "The thinking mind is not your mind," and immediately feared: "Then we are wood and stone, without a mind." Only when he received the Buddha's other teachings:

---

16 https://www.buddhanet.net/e-learning/buddhism/dp01.htm

"The pure view is the true nature," did he awaken and salute the Buddha with gratitude: "Eliminate the egoness from numberless lifetimes."

Accepting the delusions as your mind is like accepting waves as the ocean. The pure true nature is Nirvana, happiness, peace, and liberation from birthlessness. The birth and death of wind and waves is the cycle of incarnation, the world of afflictions. Beings live with false thoughts, so they suffer constantly. Buddhas and bodhisattvas return to their true nature, so their faces are always calm and fresh.

Karma binds people in ten thousand paths of reincarnation, seemingly with no way to escape. Who would have the practice that as soon as the lamp of enlightenment lit up, they immediately disappeared without a trace?

All day long, we often think like this, like that, taking thoughts as our mind, entwining ourselves in it, so it becomes majestic, chaotic, surrounding our spirit. People use tranquilizers to relieve suffering. The Partriarch Bodhidharma said: "Bring your mind here and I will give you peace." Venerable Hue Kha turned back to look for his mind and couldn't find it. Only then did he realize that his original afflictions were inherently empty. Who could bind him?

The wind represents the mental object. The wind makes the sea waves. The mental object causes consciousness to give rise to false thoughts. What is the mental object? Our mind has four characteristics: Brightness, reminding, memory, and practice. The eyes see colors, the ears hear sounds, the nose smells scents, the tongue tastes flavors, and the body feels touch. Five sense organs know five worldly objects as the brightness. the brain quietly records it as memory, forever preserving the recorded image (practice). Every time we need it, we remember it (reminding). These shadows are the mental object. Because of this, we remember many things from our childhood. Past experiences are not lost. Practitioners receive the ability to remember past stories spanning many lifetimes. The shadow of the five sense objects is stored in the storehouse consciousness (the mental object). Every time it appears, the consciousness immediately clings to distinguish calculation as a scene of existence, becoming the delusions that obscure wisdom. **The Four Foundations of Mindfulness are masters of subduing delusion.**

From numberless lives to now, beings have been reeling because of four inversions:

1. The body is impure, but we always cherish it and take it as our refuge.

2. Receiving is the suffering but still yearning, hoping to get more, better.

3. The mind is impermanent and delusional. However, we still firmly believe that it is a clear and steadfast piece of water.

4. The mental object is not real, but let's say the six internal organ senses, the six external objects, and the six consciousnesses in between are real.

By contemplating maturely, you will not be enslaved

by the six worlds and will restore your freedom and independence.

The feelings of pain and pleasure do not exist by themselves, they only arise whenever the organ senses come into contact with the external objects. Depending on the conditions, it will appear; it means it does not exist on its own. People conceive themselves to be smarter than all things, yet still like all things, their whole lives are being deceived by these illusions. Fighting each other to enjoy, killing and punishing each other to compete, cursing, tearing apart, feuding . . . in the end, it is just because of two pairs of suffering and joy, love, and hate (feeling and thinking).

We cry suffering. The Buddha called it the *suffering-suffering*, because the body is already suffering from birth, old age, illness, and death, but also suffers from the external objects.

When we are happy, the Buddha calls it the *changing-suffering* because the nature of all things is impermanent. The past is gone, the present is disappearing. Feeling happy is only because of the external object and quickly it will disappear.

When we experience neither suffering nor joy, the Buddha said it is *formation-suffering*. Because of the delusion that the senses are real, the attachment to ego and the belongings of self becomes stronger and stronger, then definitely it leads to the three suffering realms (the animal, ghost, and hell).

Practice the Four Foundations of Mindfulness, daily

reflect on your body, mind, and surroundings to calm your mind. Even if you become a monastic, you will still be deeply entangled in troubles and carry the burden for the rest of your life. Worshiping and praying to the merciful Buddhas, bodhisattvas, and sages cannot help. You must have wisdom, a true view, and a vision that is true to the truth to be able to liberate ignorance. Besides light, no divine force can destroy the darkness.

Buddhism often has the saying: "The eight winds blow without moving" to praise those who practice effectively. The eight winds are wealth, loss, destruction, humiliation, promotion, praise, criticism, sadness, and joy.

Liberation is breaking the chains of birth and death. Wisdom is to dispel ignorance, the root of samsara.

The Sutra of Forty-two Chapters narrated that one morning the Buddha went on almsround. A Brahmin was very angry, because so many his disciples had followed the Buddha. He loudly cursed the Buddha who remained silent, calm, and walked with great dignity into the village. The Brahmin shouted:

"Is the Buddha deaf?"

"No, I am not."

"Why do you not answer?"

The Buddha gently replied: "Suppose you give a gift to someone and he does not accept it, who does the gift belong to?

"I'll bring it home!"

"Likewise, if I don't accept it, your words have nothing to do with me."

The winner will face the hate

The lost can't sleep peacefully.

More or less, let go.

Be at ease.

This is an example of action that we must always remember as a guideline. Contemplation of negative words is the merit.

The speaker becomes a good and knowledgeable person. It is not due to praise or criticism that resentment arises, which is the unborn-patience power.

Venerable Hue Tich asked Zen Master Trung Ap: "What is the Buddha nature?"

"Let's give an example: The cage has six doors. The monkey outside, no matter which door he comes to, shouted "ooh ooh ah ah". The monkey inside immediately responded: "ooh ooh ah ah."

"What if the monkey is sleeping inside?"

"We see each other!"

What does it mean to ask about the Buddha's nature and the zen master answered with a story about two monkeys? The monkey outside is the six moving objects. The monkey inside is the discriminating consciousness. If you are asleep, no matter how much noise is outside, everything will be peaceful.

We are not subjected by the ourside objects,

Then the enlightenment is opened.

Return to consider the world

Just like in a dream.

Consciousness arises, attached to the six sense objects and makes us forget our awareness. The Buddha nature is revealed day and night in the six organ senses. We just need to subdue the monkey's false mind and the job will be done. The Theravada suttas call this liberation. The Mahayana sutras call this the enlightenment of the mind to see the nature of Buddhahood. Hundreds of thousands of methods all come back to this one root; there is no other way.

* * *

THE FOUR PARTS OF HUYEN TY SAO VINAYA

(The Tenth Volume, The Abbot's Duties)

The Buddha said: Bhikkhus keep the mindfulness and maintain your dignity, that is my teaching.

- What is the meaning of mindfulness?

    Contemplation of the internal body: Be diligent in maintaining it, not scattering thoughts, subduing greed and sorrow. Contemplation of the external body, contemplation of the internal and external body, contemplation of feelings, contemplation of the consciousness, and contemplation of the mental objects are the same. That way you will have the right mindfulness.

- How do you maintain dignity?

  In and out, bowing, eating, chewing, wearing clothes, standing, sitting, and speaking silently. On twelve sessions, in the four postures, practice single-mindedness in any position.

* * *

The Four Foundations of Mindfulness are not only at the top of the Sravakas Buddhist sect. From the Mahayana to the practitioners of the Teaching Perfection sect, there is not a single one who does not practice the Four Foundations of Mindfulness.

The Buddha entering Nirvana answered Anan's last question: "Bhikkhus must worship the precepts (sila) as their teacher. Not having the same precept, not co-staying in the same room, bhikkhus must practice Dharma based on the Four Foundations of Mindfulness. Without the Four Foundations of Mindfulness there is no progress."

* * *

The great Master Thien Thai Tri Gia taught: Without understanding the Four Foundations of Mindfulness, all practices are not Buddha Dharma. Only with the wisdom of the Four Foundations of Mindfulness we can one transform the negative and manifest righteousness and achieve the three Buddhist vehicles and attain the supreme bodhi.

Because of the cover of the five skandhas, we see wrongly the purity from the impure form, we feel pleased from the suffering senses; we attach ourselves in thoughts and actions and we maintain the illusion of permanence in our consciousness. If we want to correct these wrong views, we must study and practice the Four Foundations of Mindfulness.

My body is my internal body. The human body is an external body. They cooperate contemplating that mine and others are the internal and external bodies. The physical body is born from impure karma in previous lives. Karma is transferred at the consciousness, which brought us into the mother's womb, and has five impurities:

1. The impure birthplace: This body is neither a lotus flower, nor made of sandalwood. It is grown in blood and pus, next to defecation, coming out from the urinary tract.

2. The impure seed: Take two drops of the father's semen and mother's blood as the physical body.

3. The impure appearance: the thirty-two impure parts composed the body.

4. The impure nature: From exual desire and impure karma, taking the flesh desire as substance. If you do not practice contemplation methods to change, then taking all the sea water to wash will not clean.

5. The impure end period: The dead karma of ending

destiny, the body has nine boring signs:

- The dead grey
- The swelling
- The cracked ulcers
- The blood and pus spread
- The skin and flesh rot
- The maggots crawl
- Only the skeleton remains
- The body hair falls off
- Bones decay and return to the earth

* * *

The Four Foundations of Mindfulness cause unborn evil not to be born, the evil that has already arisen to be eliminated, the goodness that has not yet arisen to arise, the good that has already arisen to increase. The four right efforts, or four genuine restraints, are accomplished. The four types of concentration are called the the four bases of miraculous powers.[17] The five good bases that arise are called the five roots.[18] The five strengths that destroy the world are the five

17. The four bases of miraculous powers: Intention or purpose or desire or zeal (chanda), effort or energy or will (viriya), consciousness or mind or thoughts (citta) and investigation or discrimination (vīmaṃsā; Skt: mīmāṃsā).
18. The five roots: The roots of faith, exertion, memory, meditation, and wisdom.

powers.[19] Distinguishing the uses of the path is called the seven factors of enlightenment.[20] Practicing the path peacefully is enough for the noble eightfold path.[21] After practicing the above thirty-seven aids to enlightenment in Buddhist teachings, the practitioner can gain the state of good existence *(nāsrava-*jñāna), the contaminated of five skandhas which is called the yolk warmful Dharma.

From here, the practitioner can overcome the delusions of the three worlds.[22] The first one enters the peak position, the patience position, the first position in the world, develops the true *anāsrava*-jñāna (uncontaminated), the patience wisdoms,[23] attain the fruit of sotapanna. Progress to the end of wrong thought and attain arhatship. All are accomplished based on the Four Foundations of Mindfulness.

The sravakas, pratyekabuddhas, and bodhisattvas all study the Four Foundations of Mindfulness together, so this is the common path of the entire Three Vehicles.

19. The five powers: The powers of faith, exertion, memory, meditation, and wisdom.

20. The seven factors of enlightenment: Mindfulness, the investigation of mental objects, the energy, joy, tranquillity, concentration, and equanimity.

21. The Noble Eightfold Path: Right view, right aspiration, right speech, right action, right livelihood, right effort, right mindfulness, right concentration.

22. The three worlds: the Desire Realm (kāma-loka), the Form Realm (rūpa-loka), and the Formless Realm (ārūpya-loka).

23. Eight patiences and eight wisdoms. That is, the patience wisdoms to contemplate the Four Noble Truths (the suffering, the cause, the end of suffering, and the path leading to the end the suffering) in the realm of Desire, the Form and Formless realms. It is called the visualization of the Holy Truth.

https://phatgiao.org.vn/tu-dien-phat-hoc-online/kien-dao-k35580.html

This is the path that separates right from wrong. With the Four Foundations of Mindfulness, all dharmas become righteous. Without the Four Foundations of Mindfulness, all dharmas become evil. People who practice without the Four Foundations of Mindfulness, even if they are extremely good, will only receive the heavenly result. The heaven realm still is subjected to cause and effect and reincarnation, the Dharma fruit has no part. (The words are so painful. Anyone who wants to understand it thoroughly should read the four volumes of the Four Foundations of Mindfulness by Great Master Tri Gia in the Tripitaka, which contains a map of the Foundations of Mindfulness for both the general teaching, the special teaching and the complete teaching).

* * *

MAHA PRAJÑĀ PARAMITĀ SŪTRA

(Quảng Thừa Chapter)

The Buddha taught: Subhuti, the great vehicle of the Bodhisattva is the Four Foundations of Mindfulness.

Then Buddha recited the entire Sutta of the Four Foundations of Mindfulness. Nagarjuna Bodhisattva in Trí Độ Treatise, argued: There are people who give up their wives, children, and property for their own sake. This is a lot of internal contamination. Some people lose their bodies because of greed or lose their lives because of lust. This is a lot of infatuation with external love. There are people who are attached both inside and out. This person must contemplate the unattainable internal and external body for the mind to be rightly concentrated.

Mindfulness at the four majestic postures to destroy the body view (the root of delusion). Practicing awareness in every movement makes the mind bright, peaceful, and not confused.

To prevent the six organ senses from leading to the three poisons of greed, anger, and ignorance. The Buddha taught to monitor the breath in and out first; then when the body and mind are calm, the practice of contemplating impurity will be stable and constant, and it will be easy to enter the samadhi state. In Buddhism, the contemplation of the breath and contemplation of impurities are the gateway to the enlightenment.

There is an example in scripture:

The butcher: a practitioner. Cow: body.

A sharp knife: the wisdom.

Kill the cow: observe transforming the attachment to the body's appearance. Divide into four parts (soil, water, wind, fire): contemplate these four elements in the body. Flesh is the soil, blood is water, breath is wind and heat in body is fire.

Searching in all four parts, we do not see our ego in any part.The self is not in the four elements, the four elements are not in the self, it is just a crazy delusion that is our body and we give it a name. Use the wisdom of "contemplation on emptiness" to distinguish the four elements and the form hindrance (khandha). Then continue with the feeling, mind, and Dharma; you will enter the path.

There is another example:

The rice barn: body.

A farmer: practitioner.

The rice field: the cause and effect of the body.

Gain the rice seeds and putting them in a storage: matured causes and conditions, so one can take on a human body. Rice, sesame, beans... thirty-two parts compose the body.

The farmer opens the warehouse and sees each thing clearly. The practitioner uses his wisdom eyes to clearly see each impure part in his body.

If a smart person contemplates his present body as above, he will feel bored and open his insight. If a person has bad karma, he must contemplate the dead body (nine boring signs as mentioned above).

The practitioner realizes the beauty that was once lush and beautiful was all an illusion, deceiving the unwise. Knowing yourself is no different. If you haven't escaped this problem, how dare you respect yourself and despise others? Thus, your mind is tamed.

After five days, the body was left in the forest, the vultures and hawks dissected it. It was clear that the heart, liver, skin, and flesh were not me, not mine, but the place where the causes, sins, merit, and karma gathered, bringing us with immeasurable suffering in the rebirth samsara.

Observance of the new dead body and reflecting on the thirty-two impurities is the contemplation of impurity. The contemplation of birds and animals eating the flesh, bones falling and crumbling to the ground is the contemplation of impermanence. Observing the whole body that nothing is real of us, only due to false causes and conditions is the contemplation of selflessness. Contemplating the body like that is not a pleasant way to eliminate greed and sorrow in the world. If you can eliminate greed, all five hindrances will be gone. Like splitting a bamboo, once the first segment is split, the following segments will break. So many evil causes can be erased here.

* * *

People in the world seek happiness, but the happiness has no place to last long. The future has not yet come, the past is gone, the present does not stop, every second the thoughts arise and pass away which the Buddha called the formation of misery. Eating and drinking are to avoid hunger and thirst. Because it relieves suffering of hunger, we temporarily consider it happiness. From misery comes birth, then we receive misery coming from the outside that the Buddha called *suffering-suffering*. We feel delight when deceiving people for a while that delight and the worldly happiness which the Buddha called *the fast changement of suffering*. It is like the sense lust that takes away the precepts of the Dharma body, kills wisdom and life, and is crazy and ignorant, which people call joy.

* * *

The mind is impermanent due to arising and passing away every second. It is not self-sufficient, so it is a selfless. Due to the combination of causes and conditions, the body is created and destroyed, so it is not real. Practicing the four holy actions (Four Places of Mindfulness), breaking the four inversions, opens the door to the true form. Contemplating the four characteristics of impermanence, non-self, suffering and emptiness, one will attain the truth of suffering. Craving and the afflictions that cause suffering are called the origin. If craving and afflictions cease, it is called the end of suffering. The means to end the suffering is called *the Way*. This is the meaning of the Four Noble Truths.

So close to attain the non-ignorance (*anāsrava-jñāna*), the uncontaminated of five skandhas which is called the yolk warm Dharma (the wisdom has developed like a palm tree that feels hot). The yolk warm dharma is increased like a mountain climber gradually reaching the top, called peak position. The summit to patience position and arahantship is the full fruition of the Four Foundations of Mindfulness in the Sravaka Buddhist sect. Bodhisattva's peak is called Dharma position. The first Bodhisattva position and virtue is called the patience

Dharma. Sotapanna to arahant is the Bodhisattva's unborn patience state (anutpattika-dharma-kṣānti).[24]

Much wisdom is called the Four Foundations of Mindfulness. Diligence is called the Four Right Efforts. Having a lot of concentration is called the four bases of miraculous powers. When first practicing, mindfulness is the first step. Constantly practice in this way and the wisdom gradually comes. That is why it is not called the four Places of Wisdom but called the four Places of Mindfulness. The true essence of the Four Foundations of Mindfulness is wisdom.

* * *

THE FOUR PARTS OF VINAYA

Keeping the Great and Small Precepts

There are three levels of the Four Foundations of Mindfulness:

1. Sravakas, based on the Four Noble Truths, use the truth of suffering as the first door to practice the Four Foundations of Mindfulness (body, feeling, consciousness, and mental objects are all suffering), abandoning wrong views or thoughts or attaining for the results of sainthood.

---

24. The unborn patience state (anutpattika-dharma-kṣānti): no birth, no beginning, no birth from anything, which means it is neither real nor false. It is an absolutely non-dual state, immutable, without movement, without change.

2. Pratyeka-buddhas, relying on the twelve causes and conditions, use contemplation on the cause of misery (touching, receiving, attaching and grasping) as the first door to practice the Four Foundations of Mindfulness. They have the quick insight to transform abandoning the wrong views or thoughts, and to destroy the habits and gain the fruit of pratyeka-buddhas.

3. Bodhisattvas develop the four great vows[25] using the Eightfold Noble Path as the first door (the above two parts are to use wisdom to contemplate, while this is to use the virtue to contemplate the Four Places of Mindfulness. For example, when giving alms, bodhisattvas are awakened directly that the body is impure, the feeling is suffering, the consciousness is impermanent, the external object is selfless. This is the aim of the thirty-seven chapters to support enlightenment. Based on the six pāramitās, [26] bodhisattvas cultivate the Four Foundations of Mindfulness for three great kalpas, transforming the defilements, saving beings, maturing of virtues, and then after attaining thirty-four minds (8 patience + 8 wisdom + 18

25. The four great vows of a bodhisattva: Sentient beings are numberless; I vow to save them. Desires are inexhaustible; I vow to put an end to them. The Dharmas are boundless; I vow to master them. The Buddha Way is unattainable; I vow to attain it.
26. Six pāramitā, in Mahāyāna ("Greater Vehicle") Buddhism, any of the perfections, or transcendental virtues, practiced by bodhisattvas ("Buddhas-to-be") in advanced stages of their path toward enlightenment. The six virtues are generosity (dāna-pāramitā); morality (śīla-pāramitā); perseverance (kṣānti-pāramitā); vigor (vīrya-pāramitā); meditation, or concentration (dhyāna-pāramitā); and wisdom (prajñā-pāramitā).

emptiness),[27] they can cut off subtle ignorance.

---

27. Eight patiences and eight Wisdoms. That is, the patience wisdoms to contemplate the Four Noble Truths (the suffering, the cause, the end of suffering, and the path leading to the end the suffering) in the realm of desire, the form and formless realms. It is called the visualization of the holy truth.

https://phatgiao.org.vn/tu-dien-phat-hoc-online/kien-dao-k35580.html

Eighteen emptinesses: In the Great Prajnaparamita Sutra:

1. Internal emptiness: the six senses have no real entity; they are not me.

2. External emptiness: the six worldly objects have no real substance and are not our concern.

3. Internal and external emptiness: all twelve places have no real entity.

4. Emptiness-emptiness: all three emptinesses are ended (the medicine has cured the disease; the medicine must also be stopped).

5. The great emptiness: because the emptiness has no edge.

6. The first meaning of emptiness: the true emptiness of all dharmas.

7. The existence is empty: the causes and conditions give rise to illusion.

8. The un-work is empty: like emptiness, without form.

9. The final emptiness: no dharma is empty.

10. Beginningless is empty: using the word beginningless to show the meaning of having no beginning, but saying beginningless turns out to refer to having beginning, so it is necessary to remove the word beginningless.

11. Dissolving into emptiness: due to separation, it becomes empty. For example, if we separate the four elements (soil, water, wind and fire), our body does not exist.

12. The nature of emptiness: no real entity.

13. The self-appearance is empty: the combined appearance and the individual appearance are both empty. The human body is empty. The eyes, ears, nose, tongue, and body are empty.

14. All dharmas are empty: all phenomena are false.

15. Impossible to attain emptiness: because it cannot be grasped, we know that there is no real entity.

16. The lawless emptiness: nothingness without form.

17. The empty dharma: there is appearance but no nature.

18. Neither existence dharma, nor emptiness: no action, no condition, are all emptiness.

Both main defilements[28] and sub-defilements[29] will be ended, reaching the infinite path.

* * *

THE FOUR FOUNDATIONS OF MINDFULNESS

(Introducing an essential method)

The mind has many defilements, the root of which are the three poisons of greed, anger, and ignorance, which motivate actions and result in the retribution of reincarnation. Only arhats who have completely destroyed this pair of three have freedom in the full meaning of the liberator. The ups and downs of life, the misfortunes or luck of worldly events no longer affect those who have truly realized the pure virtue saint.

The practitioner clearly distinguishes each thought. Try to prevent bad things that have not yet arisen and get rid of them if they have already arisen. Create and develop good things that have not yet arisen, preserve and maintain if they have arisen. That is the function of the right effort. Staying away from the two extremes of sensuality and asceticism, the middle path has since ancient times brought the saints and sages to the mountaintop of liberation and insight.

Standing on a street corner, looking at passers-by, we only see the image of bustling anxiety and hardship. It is rare to see a calm, peaceful, comfortable face. The

28. Main ignorance: the worng view and thought.
29. The habit energy of afflictions remains.

restless and impatient leading to hasty decisions and less cautious words and actions.

The noisy and bustling conditions cause mental stress and harm health. The Buddha taught the bhikkhus: "While gathering, there are only two things that should be done":

a) Discuss the Dharma.

b) Silence.

The great abilities are forged and trained in silence. The silence is an essential need to keep the mind healthy. Words are silver; silence is gold.

Newspapers around the world speak out against space pollution, ocean pollution, land pollution, and so on. Buddhism has been actively purifying body, speech, and mind for 3,000 years, fighting against the mental pollution.

Vipassana meditation illuminates the four characteristics of all phenomena: impermanence, non-self, suffering, and emptiness. These strip away all illusions about the self, and thoroughly washes away all impurities of the mind. Among the Noble Eightfold Path, right view and right thought belong to wisdom. Right effort, right concentration, and right mindfulness belong to concentration. Right speech and right action belong to morality (precepts).

Mindfulness achieves both concentration and wisdom at the same time, increasing the deep and sharp capacity for right thinking and right view, which is truly an extremely essential practice for spiritual purity.

Monks, for example. If there is a crowd, growing larger and larger, loudly shouting:

"Look, this beautiful young woman is dancing and singing." A young man who really wanted to live, did not like to die, loved to have fun, and did not want to suffer, was ordered by the king to carry a bowl full of oil and walk among the crowd of people and that beautiful girl. Behind him, the executioner followed closely, sword in hand at the ready. If you spill a drop of oil, your head will immediately fall to the ground.

Hey monks, does that young man dare to be distracted and not pay attention to the bowl of oil?

- World-Honored One, definitely not.

- Bhikkhus, you must concentrate your mind and diligently rely on the four dharmas of mindfulness in the same way.

1. The contemplation of body helps us understand that the body is just an ever-changing process, not a real entity. This one-fathom-long body is just a mass of impurities that give birth to old age, sickness, and death. Scientific power with all its miracles cannot change the four sufferings of the world.

   Such a concept of life is neither pessimistic nor optimistic but simply practical. Because they know the truth, Buddhists live following reason and are often peaceful and happy.

2. In the contemplation of feelings, the awakened person focuses on happy, painful, or normal feelings. Try to objectively experience those

feelings as truth. Equanimity is not influenced by feelings, free from dependence on the senses. Not enslaved by our feelings; the right person sees clearly that they arise and die, are temporary, and have no real substance.

3. Contemplation of the mind is the work of examining one's thoughts. The practitioner tries to contemplate both the wholesome and the unwholesome, without attachment or dissatisfaction. Practitioners realize that the so-called mind is just a process that always changes according to the conditions of the dharma world and has nothing to do with the ego.

4. Since ancient times, we have always been subject to false concepts, baseless illusions, and deluded prejudices. Now the Buddha separates our nature into five aggregates to teach us to understand ourselves. Observing that each aggregate is not real, the main characteristic is impermanence.

The Buddha compared that the form is a foam, feeling is a water bubble, perception is the mist, actions are as the water hyacinth, and consciousness is a magician. The Buddha taught to observe the dangers of the five hindrances, the illusion of the organ senses, and the six worldly objects. Use the seven factors of enlightenment to train your mind to live independently, calmly with clarity and freedom. Gradually we will be able to free ourselves from the constraints of the cycle of birth and death.

We cling to things. The bondage is not in the senses or in the physical world, but in the mind. The treatment method is the Four Foundations of Mindfulness. The art of refusing to let go is a success worthy of continued and persistent effort.

There is a saying: "Sow an action to reap a habit, a habit of sincerity. Our character is the destiny of our tomorrow."

Whether we are mindful of the body, feelings, consciousness or mental objects, we must be completely objective. Because we stand outside and pay attention to the music, we can enjoy the music as it is intended rather than the musician who is worried about performance technique.

Even though we have reached a fairly high level, we still have hidden deep impurities so we cannot be absolutely pure. By following the breath, the mind becomes calm and peaceful. Now use insight wisdom to eliminate hidden unwholesomeness and wash away ignorance. Otherwise, whether sweet or bitter, the six wordly objects will stimulate them to arise, poisoning our words and actions. The five organ senses, depending on conditions and karma, cannot see things as they really are. What's more, there are still the hidden egos, love, and hate, so to the false we think it real; to misery we think it happy; to temporary, we think it permanent. Apart from precepts and concentration, we cannot attain liberation.

Not everyone has the ability to immediately attain sainthood. We should be honest in our efforts, pure in our will, and try not to falter. Our predecessors achieved a state of tranquility, peace, and joy. Regular practice and perseverance are the secret to success.

Letting the animal nature control us is the most pitiful slave. Having self-control is the one who holds the greatest power. The key to self-control is to train the mind. Digging deep into the deepest recesses of our mind requires meditation.

Suffering and happiness, good and evil, life and death, do not come to us due to the external principles. All are consequences of our thoughts, words, and actions. The complex mechanism of the mind is the core that arranges human life. Therefore, moral virtue is an extremely important factor, a rich resource, guiding the spirit to present and future happiness.

* * *

THE SRI LANKAN GREAT MASTER

Those who return to the Four Lands of Mindfulness will erase all conflicts and open a bright sky. The Four Foundations of Mindfulness is the firm belief of Buddhists in building truly human people and society.

The first attempt is to transform the five hindrances into the five limbs of meditation:

1. When equanimity arises, greed ceases.

2. When joy and happiness arise, anger will end.

3. When directed thought arises, drowsiness ends.

4. When evaluation (insight) arises, doubts disappear.

5. When one-mind arises, restlessness ceases.

All the work of listening to the Dharma, practicing the Dharma, and speaking the Dharma has only one goal: liberation. If we do not continuously pay attention to our inner self, we will not find liberation. If we eliminate all self-love and attachment, the job will be done. Clearly the Four Foundations of Mindfulness combine all three holy Dharmas.

PRECEPT – CONCENTRATION – WISDOM

If the wind of the senses is followed, it will cause storms of greed, anger, and ignorance. Greed and anger cause the mouth to speak and the body to do wrong. Delusion sees good as evil, evil as good. These three basic afflictions are both like fire that cooks and like water that engulfs.

The Buddha separates the five aggregates from afflictions like a deforester clearing small bushes without harming large trees. Whoever clears the five aggregates will enjoy peace.

Walking dignified through life without attachment is the path to Nirvana.

APPENDIX 2

PALI TIPIṬAKA CHANTING CEREMONY
IN BODHGAYA, INDIA, ON DECEMBER 2–12, 2023

(Ven. Bhikṣuṇī Gioi Huong)

The Pali Tipitaka includes the Suttas, Vinaya, and Abhidhamma written in an ancient Pali language. This is the Dhamma left for humanity by Shakyamuni Buddha, to turn suffering into peace of happiness for both monks and laypeople. The Pali Tipitaka has been translated into English, Vietnamese, and other languages.

The Tipitaka (Triple Basket) in Vietnamese is comprised of:

1. The Sutta Piṭaka consists of five sets of Nikayas (Dīgha-nikāya, Majjhima-nikāya, Saṃyutta-nikāya, Aṅguttara-nikāya, Khuddaka-nikāya).

2. The Vinaya Pitaka contains the precepts of Bhikkhus, Bhikṣuṇīs, and disciplines in the monastery.

3. The Abhidhamma Pitaka explains, analyzes, summarizes, and makes it easy to understand the Buddha's teachings in the scriptures.

The scene of great chanting under the Bodhi Tree, December 3, 2023

The Pali Tipitaka Recitation Assembly, led by Dr. Wangmo Dixey (president of the Light of Buddhadharma Foundation International (LBDFI)[30] and monks in Theravada Buddhist countries, is organized yearly at the Mahabodhi Tower, Bodh Gaya, India. This year of 2023 is the 18th International Tipitaka Chanting Ceremony, Bodhgaya, India, and is hosted by Cambodian Buddhism (Cambodia Chief Organizer). It will be rotated to every country each year.

The great Vinaya Pitaka recitation ceremony was very large with the participation of more than 4,000 monks, nuns, and Buddhists from Southeast Asian Buddhist countries such as India, Bangladesh, Lao PDR, Cambodia, Thailand, Burma, Sri Lanka, Indonesia, Nepal, Vietnam. Each country will take turns leading the Pali chanting ceremony every day.

30.https://timesofindia.indiatimes.com/city/patna/tipitaka-chant-ing-to-begin-in-bodh-gaya-on-december-/articleshow/95871041.cms

Bhikkhuni Gioi Huong
chants with the Roman Pali Vinaya

The Sutta Pitaka (the first basket of the three Pitakas) had been recited in previous years and in the year 2023 chanting of the Vinaya Pitaka (Vinaya Pitaka Parajika Pali, Pacittiyapali, Maha-Vagga Pali) began. However, because there are numerous countries and languages, the Corporate Body of the Buddha Educational Foundation (Taiwan, R.O.C.) offered to print the Vinaya in many languages such as Roman Pali, Devanagari Pali, Thai Pali, Bengali Pali, and Khmer Pali. Because of the large amount of participants and the limited area in front of the Bodhi Tree, each country set up its own tent around the Mahabodhi Tower. There is a master of ceremonies who is holding a microphone and chanting loudly in their country's language. The Buddhist Sangha of India (host) and Bangladesh arranged to chant under the Bodhi tree.

On the opening day, many Most Venerable Elders from Southeast Asian countries were present. On the government side, Mr. Ramnath Kovind (former president of India) and Governor Phagu Chauhan were the chief guests who came to give a speech. Numerous other patrons also came to the stage to congratulate the great chanting Tipitaka ceremony and warmly welcome the participants.

The daily chanting schedule was from 7 a.m. to 5 p.m. The Dhamma talks were offered alternately by the monks, and then at the end of the hour, the musical performances were given by Cambodian and Indian artists. International delegations and individuals came to make offerings at break time as well. Many delegations cooperated with the organizers to prepare food offerings such as vegetarian lunches, tea, and fruit cakes. It was very thoughtful and caring so that the participants could be free from worries to perform all-day chanting in the ceremony.

Vietnamese nuns return to attend
the Tipitaka Chanting Ceremony

On the occasion of the ten days of chanting in the Pali Vinaya ceremony, the devas and humans rejoiced as there were more than 4,000 monks, nuns, and Buddhists from Southeast Asian countries attending, including Ven. Bikkhuni Gioi Huong (Abbot of Huong Sen Pagoda, California, USA), nuns, and Buddhists from near and far, and those who have sincerely donated spending money and 3,000 suttas compiled by Huong Sen Pagoda.

Dr. Kaylan Priya Thero Mahathero and Bikkhuni Gioi Huong make offerings to the Great Monk

May the merits be rejoiced of those monks, nuns, and Buddhists from all over the world who have returned to the sacred Bodhi Tree, Mahabodhi Tower, Bodhgaya, India, together chanting the suttas and revising the precious, noble and liberated teachings of the Buddha.

We would like to sincerely thank the nuns, the Buddhists of Huong Sen Pagoda, and compatriots from near and far who have generously made offerings. A special thanks to Dr. Siri Sumedha Mahathero (Abbot of Ceylon Temple), Dr. Kaylan Priya Mahathero (Abbot of Bangladesh Temple), and Bhante Buddharatna, along with Indian Buddhists who helped with the packing of 3,000 books, as well as helping to transport all the gifts to the sacred Bodhi Tree and Mahabodhi Tower. From the bottom of my heart with full reverence, I offer this to the Great Sangha.

May the Dhamma practice of giving and offering

Be the root of happiness and blessings.

Bodh Gaya, December 3, 2023

Sincere regards,

With metta,

Bikkhuni Gioi Huong

Huongsentemple@gmail.com

Offerings to Buddha, Dhamma, and Sangha

APPENDIX 3
PHOTOS OFFERING BOOKS TO MONASTICS UNDER BODHI TREE
BODHGAYA, INDIA, IN DECEMBER 3rd, 2023

Cambodia Chief Organizer
18 th INTERNATIONAL TIPITAKA

Cambodia Chief O
NATIONAL

BẢO ANH LẠC BOOKSHELF

Dr. Bhikṣuṇī TN Giới Hương composed

1.1. THE VIETNAMESE BOOKS

1. *Bồ-tát và Tánh Không Trong Kinh Tạng Pali và Đại Thừa* (Boddhisattva and Sunyata in the Early and Developed Buddhist Traditions).

2. *Ban Mai Xứ Ấn* (The Dawn in India) - *Tuyển tập các Tiểu Luận Phật Giáo* (Collection of Buddhist Essays), (3 tập).

3. *Vườn Nai – Chiếc Nôi* (Phật Giáo Deer Park–The Cradle of Buddhism).

4. *Quy Y Tam Bảo và Năm Giới* (Take Refuge in Three Gems and Keep the Five Precepts).

5. *Vòng Luân Hồi* (The Cycle of Life).

6. *Hoa Tuyết Milwaukee* (Snowflake in Milwaukee).

7. *Luân Hồi trong Lăng Kính Lăng Nghiêm* (The

Rebirth in *Śūraṅgama* Sūtra).

8. *Nghi Thức Hộ Niệm, Cầu Siêu* (The Ritual for the Deceased).

9. *Quan Âm Quảng Trần* (The Commentary of Avalokiteśvara Bodhisattva).

10. *Nữ Tu và Tù Nhân Hoa Kỳ* (A Nun and American Inmates).

11. *Nếp Sống Tỉnh Thức của Đức Đạt Lai Lạt Ma Thứ XIV* (The Awakened Mind of the 14th Dalai Lama).

12. *A-Hàm: Mưa pháp chuyển hóa phiền não* (*Agama – A Dharma Rain transforms the Defilement*), 2 tập.

13. *Góp Từng Hạt Nắng Perris* (Collection of Sunlight in Perris).

14. *Pháp Ngữ của Kinh Kim Cang* (The Key Words of Vajracchedikā-Prajñāpāramitā-Sūtra).

15. *Tập Thơ Nhạc Nắng Lăng Nghiêm* (Songs and Poems of Śūraṅgama Sunlight).

16. *Nét Bút Bên Song Cửa* (Reflections at the Temple Window).

17. *Máy Nghe MP3 Hương Sen* (Hương Sen Digital Mp3 Radio Speaker): Các Bài Giảng, Sách, Bài viết và Thơ Nhạc của Thích Nữ Giới Hương (383/201 bài).

18. *DVD Giới Thiệu về Chùa Hương Sen*, USA (Introduction on Huong Sen Temple).

19. *Ni Giới Việt Nam Hoằng Pháp tại Hoa Kỳ* (Sharing the Dharma - Vietnamese Buddhist Nuns in the

United States).

20. *Tuyển Tập 40 Năm Tu Học & Hoằng Pháp của Ni sư Giới Hương* (Forty Years in the Dharma: A Life of Study and Service—Venerable Bhikkhuni Giới Hương), Thích Nữ Viên Quang, TN Viên Nhuận, TN Viên Tiến, and TN Viên Khuông.

21. *Tập Thơ Nhạc Lối Về Sen Nở* (*Songs and Poems of Lotus Blooming on the Way*).

22. *Nghi Thức Công Phu Khuya – Thần Chú Thủ Lăng Nghiêm* (Śuraṅgama Mantra).

23. *Nghi Thức Cầu An – Kinh Phổ Môn* (The Universal Door Sūtra).

24. *Nghi Thức Cầu An – Kinh Dược Sư* (The Medicine Buddha Sūtra).

25. *Nghi Thức Sám Hối Hồng Danh* (The Sūtra of Confession at many Buddha Titles).

26. *Nghi Thức Công Phu Chiều – Mông Sơn Thí Thực* (The Ritual Donating Food to Hungry Ghosts).

27. *Khóa Tịnh Độ – Kinh A Di Đà* (The Amitabha Buddha Sūtra).

28. *Nghi Thức Cúng Linh và Cầu Siêu* (The Rite for Deceased and Funeral Home).

29. *Nghi Lễ Hàng Ngày - 50 Kinh Tụng và các Lễ Vía trong Năm* (The Daily Chanting Rituals and Annual Ceremonies).

30. *Hương Đạo Trong Đời 2022* (Tuyển tập 60 Bài Thi trong Cuộc Thi Viết Văn Ứng Dụng Phật Pháp 2022 - A Collection of Writings on the Practicing

of Buddhism in Daily Life in the Writing Contest 2022).

31. *Hương Pháp 2022* (Tuyển Tập Các Bài Thi Trúng Giải Cuộc Thi Viết Văn Ứng Dụng Phật Pháp 2022 - A Collection of the Winning Writings on the Practicing of Buddhism in Daily Life in the Writing Contest 2022).

32. *Giới* Hương - Thơm *Ngược Gió Ngàn* (Giới *Hương – The Virtue* Fragrance Against the Thousand Winds), Nguyên Hà.

33. *Pháp Ngữ Kinh Hoa Nghiêm* (Buddha-avatamsaka-nāma-mahāvaipulya-sūtra) (2 tập).

34. *Tinh Hoa Kinh Hoa Nghiêm (The Core of Buddha-avatamsaka-nāma-mahāvaipulya-sūtra).*

35. *Phật Giáo – Tầm Nhìn Lịch Sử Và Thực Hành* (*Buddhism: A Historical and Practical Vision*). Hiệu đính: Thích Hạnh Chánh và Thích Nữ Giới Hương.

36. *Nhật ký Hành Thiền Vipassana và Kinh Tứ Niệm Xứ* (Diary: Practicing Vipassana and the Four Foundations of Mindfulness Sutta)

37. *Nghi cúng Giao Thừa* (New Year's Eve Ceremony)

38. *Nghi cúng Rằm Tháng Giêng* (the Ceremony of the First Month's Full Moon)

39. *Nghi thức Lễ Phật Đản* (The Buddha Birthday's Ceremony)

40. *Nghi thức Vu Lan* (The Ullambana Festival or Parent Day)

41. *Lễ Vía Quan Âm* (The Avolokiteshvara Day)

42. *Nghi cúng Thánh Tổ Kiều Đàm Di* (The Death Anniversary of Mahapajapati Gotami)

43. *Nghi thức cúng Tổ và Giác linh Sư trưởng* (The Ancestor Day)

1.2. THE ENGLISH BOOKS

1. *Boddhisattva and Sunyata in the Early and Developed Buddhist Traditions.*

2. *Rebirth Views in the Śūraṅgama Sūtra.*

3. *Commentary of Avalokiteśvara Bodhisattva.*

4. *The Key Words in Vajracchedikā Sūtra.*

5. *Sārnātha-The Cradle of Buddhism in the Archeological View.*

6. *Take Refuge in the Three Gems and Keep the Five Precepts.*

7. *Cycle of Life.*

8. *Forty Years in the Dharma: A Life of Study and Service—Venerable Bhikkhuni Giới Hương.*

9. *Sharing the Dharma -Vietnamese Buddhist Nuns in the United States.*

10. *A Vietnamese Buddhist Nun and American Inmates.*

11. *Daily Monastic Chanting.*

12. *Weekly Buddhist Discourse Chanting.*

13. *Practice Meditation and Pure Land.*

14. *The Ceremony for Peace.*

15. *The Lunch Offering Ritual.*

16. *The Ritual Offering Food to Hungry Ghosts.*

17. *The Pureland Course of Amitabha Sutra.*

18. *The Medicine Buddha Sutra.*

19. *The New Year Ceremony.*

20. *The Great Parinirvana Ceremony.*

21. *The Buddha's Birthday Ceremony.*

22. *The Ullambana Festival (Parents' Day).*

23. *The Marriage Ceremony.*

24. *The Blessing Ceremony for The Deceased.*

25. *The Ceremony Praising Ancestral Masters.*

26. *The Enlightened Buddha Ceremony.*

27. *The Uposatha Ceremony (Reciting Precepts).*

28. *Buddhism: A Historical and Practical Vision.* Edited by Ven. Dr. Thich Hanh Chanh and Ven. Dr. Bhikṣuṇī TN Gioi Huong.

29. *Contribution of Buddhism For World Peace & Social Harmony.* Edited by Ven. Dr. Buddha Priya Mahathero and Ven. Dr. Bhikṣuṇī TN Gioi Huong.

30. *Global Spread of Buddhism with Special Reference to Sri Lanka.* Buddhist Studies Seminar in Kandy University. Edited by Prof. Ven. Medagama Nandawansa and Dr. Bhikṣuṇī TN Gioi Huong.

31. *Buddhism In Sri Lanka During The Period of 19th to 21st Centuries.* Buddhist Studies Seminar in Colombo. Edited by Prof. Ven. Medagama Nandawansa and Dr. Bhikṣuṇī TN Gioi Huong.

32. *Diary: Practicing Vipassana and the Four Foundations of Mindfulness Sutta.*

1.3.THE BILINGUAL BOOKS (VIETNAMESE-ENGLISH)

1. *Bản Tin Hương Sen: Xuân, Phật Đản, Vu Lan (Hương Sen Newsletter: Spring, Buddha Birthday and Vu Lan, annual/ Mỗi Năm).*

2. *Danh Ngôn Nuôi Dưỡng Nhân Cách - Good Sentences Nurture a Good Manner.*

3. *Văn Hóa Đặc Sắc của Nước Nhật Bản-Exploring the Unique Culture of Japan.*

4. *Sống An Lạc dù Đời không Đẹp như Mơ - Live Peacefully though Life is not Beautiful as a Dream.*

5. *Hãy Nói Lời Yêu Thương-Words of Love and Understanding.*

6. *Văn Hóa Cổ Kim qua Hành Hương Chiêm Bái -The Ancient- Present Culture in Pilgrim.*

7. *Nghệ Thuật Biết Sống - Art of Living.*

8. *Dharamshala - Hành Hương Vùng Đất Thiêng, Ấn Độ, Dharamshala - Pilgrimage to the Sacred Land, India.*

1.4.THE TRANSLATED BOOKS

1. *Xá Lợi Của Đức Phật* (Relics of the Buddha), Tham Weng Yew.

2. *Sen Nở Nơi Chốn Tử Tù* (Lotus in Prison), many

authors.

3. *Chùa Việt Nam Hải Ngoại* (Overseas Vietnamese Buddhist Temples).

4. *Việt Nam Danh Lam Cổ Tự* (The Famous Ancient Buddhist Temples in Vietnam).

5. *Hương Sen, Thơ và Nhạc* – (Lotus Fragrance, Poem and Music).

6. *Phật Giáo-Một Bậc Đạo Sư, Nhiều Truyền Thống* (Buddhism: One Teacher – Many Traditions), Đức Đạt Lai Lạt Ma 14th & Ni Sư Thubten Chodren.

7. *Cách Chuẩn Bị Chết và Giúp Người Sắp Chết-Quan Điểm Phật Giáo* (Preparing for Death and Helping the Dying – A Buddhist Perspective).

2.BUDDHIST MUSIC ALBUMS
from POEMS of THÍCH NỮ GIỚI HƯƠNG

1. *Đào Xuân Lộng Ý Kinh* (The Buddha's Teachings Reflected in Cherry Flowers).

2. *Niềm Tin Tam Bảo* (Trust in the Three Gems).

3. *Trăng Tròn Nghìn Năm Đón Chờ Ai* (Who Is the Full Moon Waiting for for Over a Thousand Years?).

4. *Ánh Trăng Phật Pháp* (Moonlight of Dharma-Buddha).

5. *Bình Minh Tỉnh Thức* (Awakened Mind at the Dawn) (*Piano Variations for Meditation*).

6. *Tiếng Hát Già Lam* (Song from Temple).

7. *Cảnh Đẹp Chùa Xưa* (The Magnificent, Ancient

Buddhist Temple).

8. *Karaoke Hoa Ưu Đàm Đã Nở* (An Udumbara Flower Is Blooming).

9. *Hương Sen Ca* (Hương Sen's Songs)

10. *Về Chùa Vui Tu* (Happily Go to Temple for Spiritual Practices)

11. *Gọi Nắng Xuân Về* (Call the Spring Sunlight).

12. *Đệ Tử Phật*. Thơ: Thích Nữ Giới Hương, Nhạc: Uy Thi Ca & Giác An, volume 4, năm 2023.

Mời xem: http://www.huongsentemple.com/index.php/ kinh-sach/tu-sach-bao-anh-lac

159

**Diary: Practicing Vipassana
& The Four Foundations Of Mindfulness Sutta**

Tác giả: Ven. Dr. Bhikṣuṇī TN Gioi Huong

NHÀ XUẤT BẢN TÔN GIÁO
53 Tràng Thi – Hoàn Kiếm - Hà Nội
ĐT: (024)37822845
Email: nhaxuatbantongiao@gmail.com

Chịu trách nhiệm xuất bản:
Giám đốc: ThS. Nguyễn Hữu Có

Chịu trách nhiệm nội dung:
Tổng Biên tập: Lê Hồng Sơn
Biên tập: Nguyễn Thị Thanh Thủy
Trình bày: Vũ Đình Trọng
Sửa bản in: Vũ Đình Trọng

Số lượng in: 1.000 bản, Khổ: 14 x 20 cm
In tại: Công ty TNHH Sản xuất Thương mại Dịch vụ In ấn Trâm Anh,
159/57 Bạch Đằng, phường 2, quận Tân Bình, thành phố Hồ Chí Minh.
Số ĐKXB: 537-2024/CXBIPH/05-23/TG
Mã ISBN: 978-604-61-7505-6
QĐXB: 132/QĐ-NXBTG ngày 12 tháng 3 năm 2024
In xong và nộp lưu chiểu quý I năm 2024

www.ingramcontent.com/pod-product-compliance
Lightning Source LLC
LaVergne TN
LVHW050539200726
843506LV00001B/19